D1738021

IN THE PLACE OF LANGUAGE

In the Place of Language

LITERATURE
AND THE ARCHITECTURE
OF THE REFERENT

Claudia Brodsky

Fordham University Press
NEW YORK ‡ 2009

Library of Congress Cataloging-in-Publication Data

Lacour, Claudia Brodsky, 1955–
In the place of language : literature and the architecture of the referent / Claudia Brodsky.—1st ed.
p. cm.
Includes bibliographical references.
ISBN 978-0-8232-3000-6 (cloth : alk. paper)
1. Literature—Philosophy. 2. Reference (Philosophy) 3. Reference (Linguistics) 4. Semiotics and literature. I. Title.
PN54.L34 2009
801—dc22 2009003283

Printed in the United States of America

11 10 09 5 4 3 2 1

First edition

In memory of my mother,
and to Camille and Chloe

CONTENTS

ACKNOWLEDGMENTS

RATHER THAN reflecting a conclusion long foregone, the train of thought informing this book and the trilogy of works to which it belongs owes its development in no small measure to its interruption by untoward events. Even more than in writing, in life the unforeseen intervenes, and the continuation and transformation of reflection over time that any body of work requires would not have been possible for me without the endurance of certain things. In addition to those writings that never lose their power to surprise me, these are the friends and colleagues, geographically close or far-flung, whose unflagging spirit and wit (at least when it comes to buoying my own) and sincere interest in and persistent encouragement of my work, no matter how inarticulate and reluctant my attempts to describe it, have remained a generous constant, a true gift. In innumerable ways, each *sui generis*, their support afforded me the long view of things and intermittent peace of mind I have needed most; in alphabetical order, then, I express my deep gratitude to: Leslie Adelson, Eve Tavor Bannet, Angèle Bixel, Lucie Bixel, Mike Carroll, Peter Demetz, Jacques Derrida, Emily Jayne Duckworth, Madeleine Gabourin, Alexander Gelley, Willi Goetschel, Richard Goodkin, Gerhart von Graevenitz, Anita Grosz, Barbara Guetti, Kris and Hans Hansen, Walter Hinderer, Christianne Klipfel, David LaMarche, Toni Morrison, Andrés Richner, John Robinson-Appels, Lyn Roche, Adam Rosner, Edward Schiffer, Alain Toumayon, Sam Weber, Cornel West, and Laura Zinn.

I also thank the Humboldt Foundation and the Princeton University Committee on Research in the Humanities and Social Sciences for past financial support, and Helen Tartar, Eric Newman, Loomis Mayer, and Katie Sweeney for their attentive assistance at Fordham University Press.

PREFACE

Marked Change: A Brief Account

NO ONE WHO reads it will be more surprised than I that this book, which began as a study of what building is doing in pivotal works by Goethe, turned, step by step, into a theory of the referent. A skeletal chronology of its origin may serve the purpose of explaining not the surprising conclusion to which this study comes—the very purpose which the progress of the book ends up serving—but why that end was so thoroughly unexpected.

For several years I had understood that analyses of certain "mature" works by Goethe, those that composed a renewal and turning-point in his literary writing, and whose conception was, by his own appraisal, the most far-reaching, would be as difficult to complete as they were essential to the completion of what was, during those years, a book-in-progress. That book-in-progress, which grew to include studies of several other authors as I continued to teach, and write on, Goethe, had itself started out as part of another book, a footnote to whose planned introduction developed into a book. The last and least foreseeable of these three works, on Descartes, was published some years ago; the first two, substantively written, and, in parts, published, before the present study of Goethe was completed, will now be published in their entirety after it.[1]

1. From the odd chronology outlined here derives the necessity—awkward for this author—of referencing some of those separately published studies at different junctures in the argument of the present work. These references to previous publications may sometimes convey the unsettling sense of a progress in regress, and it is indeed the case that briefly noting the arguments of these related studies, rather than restating them in their entirety, was a kind of mental shorthand required for the present study to progress. Still, references

This convoluted history, confusing to read in brief, was more densely disorienting to experience at length. Regarding it in retrospect does not explain or dispel that disorientation but may at least help to indicate its basis. What now appears evident is that, even as I worked with it, my conception of the object of study to which I was first drawn, never straightforward to start with, *changed*, and this despite the fact that the object in question, while manifesting itself differently in diverse discursive contexts, remained the same. That conceptual change took place accumulatively and gradually, which is to say, long before I knew it, or recognized it as such. Completed, individual analyses of works seemed to cohere and make sense, and yet, in each instance, with, and even within, each group of works analyzed, the specific object of analysis seemed both increasingly important to the discourse of the texts investigated *and* increasingly different from itself, a development which, by any logical measure, made no sense, or at least defied coherent, conceptual, or theoretical description.

My continuing work on Goethe, rather than completing or countermanding this change, pushed it, as the expression goes, "over the edge," or, to use the conventional hermeneutic figure, off the ever-receding horizon that always accompanies and delimits the understanding of historical phenomena in the present. For Goethe's were literary texts in which the verbal manifestations of a certain nonverbal occurrence, a kind of discursive recourse appearing at once necessary and extraneous to discourse, were most conspicuously self-evident—composed and located right on the surface, so to speak, of the stories they told—yet what the unmistakable clarity of their presentation brought me to was a kind of wall, a sense of ignorance, or at least bafflement, as to "what" they were, i.e., why they were, and what they were doing, in plain cognitive sight.

---

to these previous analyses may serve not only to indicate their direct contribution to the development of the present work, opening the angle of its own analytic movement to wider compass, but also to suggest the substantial change that contribution has already effected upon those studies themselves, altering the course of their own integration into the larger works of which they are a part.

Thus my study of Goethe wrenched the original problem or question my work had addressed back to its own beginning. That original problem arose with my perception of a kind of textual presence whose usefulness within each text—a practical function so fundamental to its integral composition as to become nearly invisible in the text, even when most explicit—could only be explicated, if at all, starting from the conceptual and imaginative premises of the very text it served. I was unable to understand, let alone explain, the tacit persistence of something indicated within individual texts as if constituted both within them and outside any text, something that, while essential to the very formation and development of each text, was itself specifically *not* a textual form.

All I knew about this appearance was that it was not another literary device, uncatalogued only because ignored, and all I didn't know took, over and over, the form of the same unspoken question: Why do many of the most transformative literary and philosophical works in the western tradition, discursive works whose art and theory change how and even what it is we understand, so often refer to, indeed often openly depend upon, nondiscursive, and nonpictoral, architectonic and architectural form? Why does a form defined by its nonfigural status and physical stasis appear critically and imaginatively necessary to texts that mark an historic change, not only in their own discursive field—in how we conceive that field and, intertwined with it, and with each practitioner's particular forms and aims, *the fact of discourse itself as given formal medium*—but in our ability to conceive, in memorable, historical form, events we ourselves observe and undergo? The fact that many of the works, in which reference to the architectonic and architectural appeared essential to the constitution of the works themselves, contradicted, at least in part, the function and effects of that referencing in others, suggested to me that I had either read too little or too much—more, in any event, than my original conception of this textual occurrence could contain. When, eventually, it became difficult for me to tell the difference between too much and too little, the very manner in which I understood "architectonic" and "architectural" changed instead: these appeared no longer loosely interchangeable descriptive terms but as the names of a single nonrepresentational form having two contradictory functions, each of which was fundamental to the purpose of articulate understanding. And in that contradiction lay the change in my own understanding of the discursive appearance of architectural form, a movement from a *pure formalism* to the *form of historicity.*

The two views composing this contradiction coincided with, without canceling, each other. They involved, on the one hand, the perception of the architectural as architectonic, an independent, self-containing form whose necessary externality to discourse made its pivotal inclusion in discourse all the more critical, and, thus, in itself significant; and, on the other, that of the architectural as the material form which, concretely, individually, renders temporality perceptible, in that, rather than theoretically setting time aside as a given, necessary if hypothetical (or "a priori") form of sensory perception and intuition—a synthetic component, with space, of a representationally limited theory of cognition—it instead serves to substantiate time by way of a certain transformation of material givens into something else, something of practical use. Precisely by subsisting in time, such a form materializes temporal difference, further allowing, *as matter individuated by action*, the discretely historical to come into view.

Thus a project that began, with Kant, as an investigation of discursive references to logical, or self-defining, structures that appear as if ex nihilo in literature and philosophy—temporally impervious *architectonic* structures both distinct from, and comprehending of, the metamorphic discourse that represents our partial experience of the world—became the study of indications of and meditations on *architecture* that neither structures nor represents but rather demarcates experience on earth. Such demarcation does not "take place" figuratively "within" language but rather, as indicated by language, on and under the material ground on which we stand. That is to say, it takes place—in the "literal" or concrete sense—where language has no proper place, within the material itself, and in so doing, it both "takes the place of" language and installs language on earth, providing a place for language to provide the "grounds" for history, for good and for ill, in the material world.[2] Alternately occasioning

2. Rousseau's seminal analysis of the role of language in "grounding" territorial appropriation, the exclusion of language from and resulting re-mystifi-

and compelling cognition and thinking, these earthly demarcations indicate what remains available for understanding even as the faces and forms of what they mark appear forever gone, destroyed by the implacable activity of humanity and nature over time.

Architecture as the mark of temporal activity that allows us to call such activity historical, rather than as an architectonic, synchronic, internally self-defining and encompassing structure, became the focus, then, of a separate study, beginning with Hegel, and it was in reading the discursive arc of architectural activity displayed in Goethe from within that altered conceptual context that I stumbled, somewhat startlingly, upon a form of marking I had not considered as related to the architectural at all.

That form is the form of the referent, of demarcation rather than signification, and of the referent as neither given in nature nor by thought—each equally impossible[3] derivations—but made. The making of reference through architectural activity of some kind, the forming of a place to which perception returns, on which imagination lingers, and language renders its "own,"—that is, both inherently *and* externally, or historically, significant—is the story that

---

cation of territorial appropriation by Carl Schmitt, and Kant's translation of Rousseau's first (negative) principle, that "the ground belongs to no one," into a positive legal theory of the necessarily artificial constitution of any claim to external possession, including in times of war, are among the placements and displacements of language in referentially based political theory discussed in section 2 of the Introduction.

3. —the one being either logically impossible or entirely fictional, since nature, having no correspondence to language, can be objectively identified only by way of language (hence the insoluble problem of sufficient definition), and the other being logically transparent but essentially circular, since any referent defined only by thought would also correspond only to that definition, making the referent not a referent but yet another product of language alone (hence the made-up objects, bearing overtly nonsensical names and taking part in science fiction–like scenarios, that routinely dominate analytic models for defining the referent). I have discussed analytic theories of the referent as linguistic convention, in Lewis, Quine, and Kripke, and the logical impasses and problem of historical uncertainty that even such differing uses of convention theory to define a law of referentiality consistently reveal, in Brodsky, "The Temporality of Convention."

shapes the dramatic and prosaic plots of Goethe's *Faust* plays and *Wahlverwandtschaften*. A visibly and literally unremarkable scene, recorded in another, partly visual medium, may serve as the most explicit, if negative, introduction to the earthly construction of the referent that Goethe's texts in specific and literature in general *represent*. For literary texts can bring to mind that which is never present to those whom it immediately affects, demarcations that, unlike changing nominal locations, are the material signs of history itself, which is to say, of the striving for language not only to designate places but materially to "take place," the very signs that revisionist attempts "to write" history work most effectively to conceal. It is to a little noted, artificially constructed and recorded scene in which such concealment is at once verbally and deictically revealed, that these prefatory remarks on the making of the referent proceed.

IN THE PLACE OF LANGUAGE

INTRODUCTION

Signs of Place

1. Referent and Annihilation: "*X*" Marks the Spot

THERE IS A MOMENT in Claude Lanzmann's *Shoah* that stands, strangely, alone. *Shoah*, a cinematic document without equal, by reason of the unthinkable acts and experiences it records, intersperses filmed verbal accounts of events participated in and witnessed with long shots of natural landscapes and sites of human engineering: cities, towns, individual buildings, train stations, lines of trains, lines of track, and the remains of extermination camps, of walled ghettos, of mass burial pits, and extermination chambers. Often it shows the merging of landscape with these, as that which already existed and was employed, and that which was expressly built, for the purpose of the daily reduction to nothing ("Ver*nicht*ung") of tens of thousands of men, women, and children of every age, state, and condition, appeared overgrown with vegetation or returned to its previous, conventional use.

The moment I have in mind has remained in my mind from my first viewing of Lanzmann's film. Extraordinarily brief, it immediately combines, like no other sequence in the four-part documentary, the verbal with the physical, contextual record. Standing a few yards away from the train station at Sobibór, on open, grass-covered ground interrupted only by parallel sets of tracks, Lanzmann, who has been speaking in front of the station with a longtime resident of Sobibór, points to the ground, defines what he is pointing to, and asks for confirmation of what he has said and done. "Here" [*Ici*], he says pointing to land abutting one set of tracks, one is "inside the camp" [*à l'interieur du camp*]. His interlocutor, looking down at the designated spot, confirms, yes. Moving some feet toward the train station and a second set of tracks, Lanzmann points down again:

"Here," he says, one is "outside the camp" [*à l'exterieur du camp*]. His interviewee and guide looks at this spot, too, and once again confirms, yes.[1]

What Lanzmann creates and records in this scene is a pure moment of reference. No narrative is delivered at this moment, nor is any particular place imaged or panned in silence on the screen. There is Sobibór, with its sign designating the town and train stop, and there are residents of Sobibór who lived "then" and live now, but there is no structural evidence of "then," of "what" happened for years in Sobibór, none of the material structures that enabled "this" to happen, day in, day out. There is now no extermination camp at Sobibór. And in pointing instead to presently imaginary boundary lines, suggested only by the ongoing presence of everyday railroad tracks, in designating "here," in one spot, and "here," in another, Lanzmann compels us to "see" what is no longer, what it was preferred that in Sobibór no one see any longer, just as, in the only ways that mattered at the time, no one "saw" it then, including especially those who saw "it" all.

This is terrible achievement enough, lucid and grim enough, but it is only the beginning or pretext of what Lanzmann does. In asking a witness to identify and distinguish "here" from "here," where no lasting distinction on and in the earth exists, to distinguish "inside" from "outside" where no wall, no enclosure now produces these and divides them, to distinguish the grounds of the comings and goings

1. Lanzmann, *Shoah*, Part One. As is often the case when his interviewees are Polish- or Hebrew-speaking, and cannot, or choose not to speak in either French, German, or English, Lanzmann speaks here (or rather "here") in French, his words, and those of his interlocutor, translated immediately by an interpreter who is with them. The following comments, focusing on Lanzmann's singular effort here to constate a "scene" of historical demarcation where no such scene exists, do not aim to speak to his documentary methods as a whole, from whose characteristic practices of extensive site viewing and insistent interviewing this passing moment is constitutively—verbally, graphically, and cinematographically—distinct, but rather to the power of such a conspicuously staged and recorded "scene" to illuminate precisely by its negative force as counterexample the writing of building as necessary marker of historical existence in fictional and theoretical texts.

of life from the grounds and factory of the manufacture of death, Lanzmann more horribly indicates that between these two there may indeed remain no perceivable difference: no perceivable difference between ongoing, small-town living and highly mechanized, technologically and so repetitively unlimited murder. Without articulating or showing the consequences of either this demarcation, of "inside" from "outside," or its obliteration, Lanzmann indicates that, at any time, there may be nothing left to differentiate between common, trodden ground and ground from which all perceptible traces of murder were likewise and repeatedly removed by enslaved laborers themselves slated for extermination, so that thousands of their fellow victims, charged with the official fiction of a few selected possessions and in possession of their natural senses, entered at regular intervals, blinder than the blind, into that "interior" they were told would cleanse them and prolong their chance to work and live and was instead, and in fact, the chamber of their death, from which the only "workers" to exit would be those charged with carrying their corpses. What Lanzmann demonstrates as he speaks and points at otherwise indistinguishable pieces of ground is that the difference between "Sobibór" and "Sobibór," between "inside" and "outside," between organized, routinized extermination and routine life, may become as undemonstrable as the difference between railroad tracks and railroad tracks, crabgrass and crabgrass.

For on the face of it, on the face of the earth, there remains no such distinction. Only the documentary director's direction of our attention to one spot, and to another, each like the other, each fully open to the light of day, and the confirmation of his verbal definition of each of these by one who knew and remembers their now eradicated referents—only this staged confluence of fleeting, circumstantial conditions, transposed onto the unearthly medium of film, yields *the* referents on which everything depended: "inside" and "outside."[2] This moment of pointing to and identifying with language what is

2. By contrast, the ontological conflation of "inside" and "outside," conceived in the service of an identification of ontology and politics under the politically annihilating aegis of "biopolitics," is discussed in this Introduction, section 3.

no longer extant, a pointing capable, therefore, of indicating only spots of emptiness, verbally localized absences of demarcation that fix in their very vacancy both eye and mind, functions, on the one hand, like a mere verbal aside, or incidental footnote, to the full-length footage of interviews and narrations, both over-filled and impossible ever to fill with detail, and, on the other, like a rudimentary topographical appendage to the mute images of abysmally incongruous *Tatorte* filmed by Lanzmann at purposefully, achingly slow pace: the lush, undulating riverbanks, thick forests and meadows of Chelmno, and the surrounding farms, streets, and homes that appear to have undergone only superficial change since the Middle Ages; excruciatingly detailed, cross-sectioned models of the two-tiered "crematoria" filled to capacity during a typical use cycle, densely packed masses of sculpted simulacra of victims progressing from chamber to chamber to death; the snow-covered, sunken remains of these chambers, and the hulking, standing entrance tower of Auschwitz, terrible imitation of the traditional medieval *Tor*. Compared with all that *Shoah* does show, the silent places and speaking persons it records, this moment of attention directed to otherwise nondescript pieces of ground appears as negligible as it is prescient.

For, in the long view, the view that both calls for and effortlessly defeats, by sheer persuasive power of the present, the immediacy of the reality artificially confirmed by documentary film-making and archival documentation—the view that encompasses the moment when those who lived on past certain death, and the structures they hardly survived the "inside" of, are no longer upon this earth, no longer standing, or speaking, no longer bodily visible, no longer living—in this view Lanzmann's indication of the already invisible, his pedantic insistence on defining precisely where life continued and stopped, foresees the possibility of real material erasure, whether natural or intended, and the obstinacy of language, and of the earth that is not language, that haunts all such obliteration. In a ghostly moment of designation, "'here,'" the moment of indicating a referent on earth, Lanzmann not only indicates, in the most uncanny of manners, the physical rather than metaphysical, concrete rather than conceptual location of life and death. He also indicates that any indication of the referent must distinguish one "'here'" from another "'here'" as inherently ungrounded language alone cannot: language which, possessed of the word ("'here'") and *not* the place ("here"), has the inherent capability to say "here," and mean it, *anywhere*; language which includes and provides place names exactly as compensation for its inherent *in*ability to link words and places. Finally, in repeating and redefining a single word in two otherwise imperceptible places, Lanzmann marks the difference between what we would otherwise conceive, according to the logical categories afforded by language, as definitionally incomparable: the difference—normally, or perhaps only nonhistorically, requiring no referential distinction—between action and matter, genocide and countryside.

In this moment, a pure moment of reference because void of any particular, referential object, Lanzmann constructs a referent where all referents have been erased. The terms written upon that erasure—itself a kind of second murder, the conscious, organized erasure of the conscious, organized erasure of life from earth—are architecturally given. "Inside" and "outside" the camp are the referents Lanzmann points to, and, because all has been made "outside" now, he points as much to the insubstantiality and essential, critical significance of language with regard to knowledge, as to the essential, material relationship of architectural activity to history, and the effacement of the historical that eradication of building entails. In composing the conditions for the indication of a referent that no longer exists, and filming that nonexistence, Lanzmann records, in this small moment, the enormity of irreplaceable, inalterable loss.

What is lost, the referent of that loss, cannot be seen in Lanzmann's first "'here,'" or second "'here,'" or anywhere, nor could it ever be, even if—implausibly but never as implausible as the history they would represent—several million life-sized, biographically accurate sculptures of human figures, depicted in the course of being hounded by the thousands into the commensurate number of thousands of historically accurate "cleansing room"/"crematoria," and providing thereby a synchronically visible representation of both the quantitative *and* qualitative magnitude of the referent, were erected in their place. Instead, pointing, with language, at a place that is nothing in particular, signifying without showing the loss that is every specific, individual death, and, with the individual, every moment, equally inexhaustibly representable, of every life stopped from continuing, every act of conscious and unconscious sensation lost forever with that life, every thought left unmemorialized, Lanzmann's "'here'" indicates the infinity that is "a" human life, an infinity indicated, rather than represented, in the finite form of the referent.

2. Theory of Appropriation: Rousseau, Schmitt, and Kant

COMPLEMENTARY TO Lanzmann's need to know where the artificial boundary dividing the life of life from the life of death once lay—a boundary which, necessitated, installed and enforced by a plan to rewrite and erase human history, leaves no trace of itself in nature in the wake of that plan's own demise and physical erasure—is the historical theory of property formation, and contradiction of any so-called natural right to property, developed by Rousseau. As for Lanzmann, so for Rousseau, a verbal act of deixis—a designation, "'here'"—is essential to any founding act of division and appropriation, and any understanding of the arbitrary nature of such origins depends, in turn, on our ability to recognize its "grounding" not in nature but language. The landmark first sentence of Part Two of Rousseau's *Second Discourse*—"The first man who, having enclosed a plot of land, thought to himself to say: 'This is mine,' and found people simple enough to believe him, was the true founder of civil society"[3]—stands as the most concise statement

3. Rousseau, *Discours sur l'origine*, p. 222: "*Le premier qui, ayant enclos un terrain, s'avisa de dire:* Ceci est à moi, *et trouva des gens assez simples pour le croire, fut le vrai fondateur de la société civile.*" Unless otherwise indicated, all translations from the French throughout this study are my own.

Anne-Lise François' remarkable *Open Secrets*, published after the completion of this manuscript, contrastively compares Rousseau's account of "the act of taking possession of a territory and declaring it 'mine'" with a kind of "pointing that would give notice of an unrealized *x* and, just as surely and swiftly, put it inevitably 'off limits,' beyond development" (36). As embodied in "the invisible artistry of the eco-activist" François compellingly describes, such non-appropriative marking characterizes the minimally differentiating

of both the wholly artificial, causally and logically ungrounded nature of the act of ascribing language to a delimited place, and the conventional, indeed regulatory status subsequently granted its function when language is credited as the proper basis for appropriation. Rousseau's mise en scène of the differentiating origin of civilization from nature stages a first, empirically directed act of human consciousness as demonstrative not only of the self-evident, and historically buried, fact that language in itself takes no place and so relies on architectural demarcations to distinguish one place from another, but that such establishment of the referent ("*Ceci est . . .*")—a linguistic act of place-taking exerting no physical force upon a made enclosure—marks and defines place not as it exists in itself, if indeed it could so exist, but rather *as* referent, thereby planting the seeds (or the semantic means) of the double history of "civil society" and "despotism" (i.e., the "sanctioning of sovereign authority by divine right") to come.[4]

As the foregoing reference to Rousseau's analysis of territorial appropriation and governance as formative while arbitrary linguistic act—integral not only to the *Second Discourse* but to Rousseau's entire corpus, from the early *Essay on the Origin of Languages* through the final *Rêveries*—and the larger analysis of architectural and linguistic place-making developed in the present work should make evident, this study includes an implicit critique of the mythologizing

---

conservation method practiced by *Earth First!*, whose nearly static method of setting aside, by spiking and selectively flagging, individual trees dissuades clear-cut logging by mere force of implication, i.e., the undemonstrable suggestion that any number of "surrounding trees" were also if not equally conspicuously spiked (36–37). By underscoring, rather, the entirely *fictional while visible* artistry of appropriation described by Rousseau, this study at once supports François' larger thesis regarding the enduring "open secrets" informing romantic literature in its nondialectical aspect, and suggests that occulted nonrepresentational marking—marking that is as inessentially grounded as it proves essentially referential in effect—constitutes the basis and informs the development of dialectical and differential understandings of history as well.

4. Rousseau, *Discours sur l'origine*, pp. 254–57. A fuller examination of the *Second Discourse* is offered in the final chapter of my *Writing, or Building* (forthcoming).

of the rule of place-taking as primordial political reality—indeed, of the very rule of myth over the polis Rousseau had demystified—that returned to prominence in the twentieth century in the notion of the *nomos* espoused by Carl Schmitt. That Schmitt's exclusively spatial theory of the state, ultimately inferring constitutional from supposedly autochthonous territorial rule ("The nomos is . . . the immediate shape, in which the political and social ordering of a people becomes *spatially* visible, the first measurement and division of the pasture, i.e., land-taking, and the concrete order that *lies within it* as well as follows from it") and obliterating the marking of temporal difference critical to any reflection on the "facts" of territorial appropriation and colonization (the same "facts," "*normative Kraft des Faktischen*," or "*faits accomplis*," which is to say, imposed fabrications, lent a similar air of inevitability by their current appellation, "facts on the ground") through an equation of past and present legitimating orders (the constituted and constitutive orders, *ordo ordinatus* and *ordo ordinans*) deriving at all moments from the single sovereign principle of *Landnahme* (land-appropriation), and both of these from a tautological assertion, of "order and place" born mystically of "earth" and of "earth" as the "mythical" "mother" of rule, should enjoy, at the time of this writing, an intellectual adherence unparalleled since Schmitt's adherence to the regime of National Socialism, may say more about current cultural mythology, our own mimetic embrace of a proclaimed "age of terror" as if of mother earth, than Schmitt's anti-theoretical conflation of legal theory with a myth of earth-power as of politics with a theosophy of divine power.[5] When Schmitt condemns Hölderlin's translation of *nomos* in Pindar by *Gesetz* ("law") as "leading to the path of error," he gives voice to the sway of this conflation over his own ability to understand that which does not conform to it, stating that Hölderlin thinks *nomos* as "law" "*even though* he knows that the law is strict mediability," that is, that the poet takes *nomos* to mean the opposite, and to take the opposing discursive form, of the lawless idea of *nomos* Schmitt asserts: "the

5. See Schmitt, *Der Nomos*, pp. 39–40, 42, 78, 13, 51 (emphasis added). Unless otherwise indicated, all translations from the German throughout this study are my own.

nomos . . .is the full immediacy of a power of right *unmediated by laws* . . . , an act of *legitimacy*, to which the legality of mere law first grants sense."[6]

Whatever the basis of Schmitt's failure to consider the poet's own considered endowment of "law" with "sense," in linkages of earthly with mortal measure through the difficult mediations of language and building, and whatever the duration of the interpretive failures of our own cultural moment—the turn from the necessary difficulties of discursive reflection on the relation of the political to the ethical and on the complex relation of these to epistemology and representation, toward an elemental creed of "legitimacy" originating instead in nature's own demotic rule (including, by unblinking extension, that of those powers who assume to speak for it)—the most incisive refutation of a radical legal conservatism whose ascription of absolute power to earthly dominion derives precisely from its foreclosure of thinking the political may be found in the language-based, contra-Hobbesian political theory of Rousseau, even at the risk of assimilating the far more complex theory of Hobbes to that of its ideological posterity in Schmitt.

Still, given that Rousseau, and his critical *Nachfolge*, Kant, are central to the present analysis of language bound, by building, to the earth, Schmitt's specific references to Rousseau and Kant merit a measure of closer scrutiny. Schmitt makes no reference in *Nomos der Erde* to Rousseau's signal demystification of a mythical conception of *Landnahme*; but he does refer to Rousseau's conceptually revolutionary redefinition of war, in *On the Social Contract* (Bk. I, Chap. IV), as "une relation d'État à État" ("a relation of state to state"), categorizing and dismissing the concept of statist war, however, as mere "wordplay" [*Wortspiel*] with the phrase, "état de guerre," that is indeed employed (two paragraphs earlier) by Rousseau in the course of a disproof of the false notion of war as "private" or "man-to-man."[7] Of the significance of this imputed *Wortspiel* to the whole of Rousseau's social thought, Schmitt states summarily: "That is indeed

6. Ibid., p. 42 (emphasis added).

7. See Rousseau, *Du contrat social*, pp. 46–47.

the whole argument."[8] Thus the founding theory of the contractual state, including one's "right" "to disobey" any "government" that has "usurped the sovereignty [of the contracting people]," and so to withdraw from such a government's war, is reduced by Schmitt to the status of a meaningless homonym; and one can judge, from this explicitly irrational view, be it of the range of meanings of "état" in French (equivalent to that of "state" in English), or, as stated, of Rousseau's "whole argument," that it was not only the false premise of property outlined in the *Second Discourse*, but Rousseau's searing critique of the inherently "antisocial" or self-"contradictory" premise of any state united with the Church of Rome—its confusion of the duties and rights of the "citizen" in this world, in which the people are sovereign, with those of the "devout" whose reward by a greater power in an afterworld is decided *for* them by that power's princes in this world, a confusion "plac[ing] man in contradiction with himself"—that Schmitt found worthy of occlusion in Rousseau.[9]

Occlusions of another kind occur in Schmitt's references to Kant, to whom Schmitt attributes an originary adherence to the notion of *Landnahme* by fact of the title of §12 of the *Metaphysik der Sitten*: "The first acquisition of a thing can be no other than that of the ground."[10] It is in this subsection of the *Metaphysik*, however, and one other (§16) to which Schmitt refers, that Kant states the basis of his subsequent deduction, following Rousseau, of the "state of citizenry" as the only possible "accordance of the free and arbitrary will of one with that of the freedom of everyone," that of "a general, really united legislative will" (§14–15).[11] This premise, to which Schmitt does not refer, is stated and restated by Kant as follows: "The earthly ground [*Boden*] belongs to no one" (§12); "All men

8. Schmitt, *Der Nomos*, p. 122.

9. Rousseau, *Du contrat social*, Bk. II, Chap. X, "On the abuse of government and its tendency to degenerate," p. 125; Bk. IV, Chap. VIII, "On civil religion," p. 175.

10. Kant, *Werkausgabe*, VIII: 372: "*Die erste Erwerbung einer Sache kann keine Andere als die des Bodens sein*."

11. Ibid., VIII: 374–75.

are originally in *common possession* of the ground of the entire earth (communio fundi originaria)" (§16).[12]

Kant's argument that a constitutional framework must accompany the social claim of anyone to possess anything external [*etwas Äusseres*] (see esp. *Metaphysik der Sitten*, §8) accords in turn with his exposition of the principles of war.[13] These are, first, that "a war of punishment (bellum punitivum)" is itself a contradiction, in that it entails "a relationship of an imperial power to subordinate powers" that is specifically "not the relationship of states among each other" (§57); second, that war, since "under governance of the state," prohibits "plunder," i.e., the taking of that which, by legal agreement among them, belongs to persons (§57); and third, that, just as the very notion of an "unlawful or unrightful enemy" (singled out by Schmitt as especially intriguing in Kant) is in itself merely "pleonastic," since "the state of nature," which it is the "expressed will" of such an enemy to "render eternal" is the very "state of unlawfulness or unrightfulness" that is perpetual war (§60), so, finally, even a war of "free peoples" against a purported "unlawful enemy" bent on eternalizing the unlawful state of nature can "*not*" be predicated upon the premise of *Landnahme*, the eventual division and rule, or "*divvying up of his land*" (§60).[14] Schmitt does note the last of these principles, but attributes his a priori rejection of the appropriation and apportionment of land through war to the "greatness and humanity of Kant," whose "philosophical ethics" he consequently allies with "theology"—the declared domain of his own political theory—rather than the "study of law": "[Kant] is not a legal scholar and stands closer to theologians than to legal scholars."[15]

However, Kant's statements that, on the one hand, "the first acquisition can only be that of the ground," i.e., that the earthly basis of acquisition, as "the thing itself," must precede that of any "mobile"

12. Ibid., VIII: 378: "*Alle Menschen sind ursprünglich in einem* Gesamt-Besitz *des Bodens der ganzen Erde*" (emphasis in text).

13. Ibid., VIII: 365–66.

14. Ibid., VIII: 470, 471, 473–74, 473 (emphasis in text); see Schmitt, *Nomos*, p. 141.

15. Schmitt, *Der Nomos*, p. 143.

"objects" acquired or "destroyed" upon it, while, on the other, that the land of another is not to be taken either as an object of acquisition or subject of colonization, follows less from Kant's own "humanity" and purported proximity to theology than to his critical deduction of the a priori form of space in the *Transcendental Aesthetic* of the *First Critique*.[16] That deduction is the first necessary to any epistemology for Kant because space is that which, like the ground in legal terms, can never be reduced to, but without which there would be no sensory intuitions of, particular objects, and which, again analogous to the original "common possession of the ground," is "transcendental" and a priori exactly because it "belongs to no one" in particular, just as it makes possible, but depends on no, particular representation. Similarly, Kant's derivation of "natural right," as opposed to legal, constitutional right, from the mere duration of one's ("chance") placement on earth, parallels his deduction, via the perception of change, of the a priori form of time (§13).[17] In describing the ground as originally belonging to no one; as the first "thing" of acquisition; *and* as that which cannot be made one's own by war, Kant, moreover, links his cognitive theory with the social theory of Rousseau, repeating in spatial and terrestrial terms the argument in *On the Social Contract* against the alienation by man of the basis of being man—not the property he has acquired but his "freedom," including, by historical extension, that of the supposed right of a parent to enslave, as if he or she were his "natural" property, a child.[18]

It is the recognition of property of any genre as an artificial or non-natural acquisition that underwrites both Rousseau's revolutionary analysis of the founding of "civil society" and Kant's attempt to base the law of civil society in the equally artificial expression of a "general, really united will," a constitutional contract that would articulate "the freedom of everyone." Anything but "mere wordplay," the resulting concept of war as between "states" rather than individuals, let alone as a state of nature identified with the powerful persuasions of myth, indicates in the first instance that war waged

16. Kant, *Werkausgabe*, VIII: 372.
17. Ibid., VIII: 373.
18. Rousseau, *Du contrat social*, Bk. I, Chap. IV, "De l'esclavage," p. 46.

merely in the name of and without the assent of the people that compose the state contradicts the "united will" expressed in law, and is lawless at its core. Yet it further implies that a war waged against *a people rather than a state* is no war but what we have come to call genocide, which, like inter-generational slavery, requires more than a supposed primordial right to territorial acquisition. A war not upon the property or place of a people but upon a people themselves, a war upon life carried out among the living, requires a verbal and architectural division of the living from the living, which enables the appropriation of something anterior to property, and the "land" or "ground" on which property rests. Before and aside from all proprietary geography, it requires, rather, the appropriation of people, of their ungrounded right to live, and thus of their death.

3. "Sovereignty" over Language: Of Lice and Men

IN THE DISCURSIVE TERMS borrowed from Lanzmann's demonstration of the arbitrary and absolutely decisive nature of the constitution of the referent, "here"—in the Introduction to an analysis of its complex literary representation by Goethe—is the "place" to acknowledge the obvious, that which Lanzmann's filmed empirical research makes discretely and, because discretely, grotesquely evident, and that is the powerful opposition between his indication of the insuperable, *if later imperceptible*, difference in meaning and experience that can correspond, at any particular moment in history, to the built difference between "inside" and "outside," and Giorgio Agamben's sovereign conflation of the two under the twin names of the "sovereign" and *bios*, the latter first distinguished, via Aristotle, only to be rendered indistinguishable by Agamben from *zōon*.[19] Still, because it is so often the obvious that escapes us, like Kant's "ground" that "belongs to no one," once terms of analysis, akin to so many pieces of earth, are appropriated, that opposition is well worth articulating, lest the sovereign division of "inside" from "outside" as of life from death be buried by an equally sovereign annihilation of any difference between them. For, while one can appreciate the authenticity of Agamben's horror at the "decadence" of "modern democracy," his equation of "modern totalitarianism" with "the society of mass hedonism and consumerism" under the unfortunate rubric, "biopolitics" (a neologism carried so far beyond as to destroy its original investment with meaning by Foucault, and whose false synthesis, in the all-encompassing scope equated with it by Agamben, is already

19. See esp. Agamben, *Homo Sacer: Sovereign Power and Bare Life*.

parsed, and contradicted, again, by Agamben's model philosopher, Aristotle—not to speak of every philosopher since Plato who has considered the uncertain dynamics of relations among men), may be (with Kafka, we can only hope) the summit of the very "decadence" Agamben abhors, that is, the objectification, in purported theoretical form, of routinized *Vernichtung* as routine for the human animal, an object of horror, yes, but one already rendered as inevitable as "the perfect senselessness" of "the society of the spectacle" by the relationship of human to animal in the fact of the human animal.[20]

Now, another word for that relationship may just be "language" (following, once again, Aristotle and any philosopher who has reflected on the human), but, as primary evidence of that relation, rather than means of its eradication, language provides little meaning to Agamben, whose method of selective quotation cites and juxtaposes bits of old and new language considered theoretically dispositional only to more effectively leave the semantic complexity and contextual historicity of language as such behind. The complementary converse of that instrumental citational method is a flattening rhetoric of repetition carried out in a drumbeat of reiterated equations, foremost among them that of "inside" with "outside." ("The sovereign power is this very impossibility of distinguishing between outside and inside, nature and exception, *physis* and *nomos*. The state of exception is . . . a complex topological figure in which not only the exception and the rule but also the state of nature and law, outside and inside, pass through one another. It is precisely this topological zone of indistinction . . . that we must try to fix under our gaze.")[21] While such passages helpfully indicate the importance of nonlinguistic, architectural form to a totalizing, alinguistic equation of human to animal, they also serve to enforce those hymnal evocations of being passing for a theory (to end all theories) of being—oxymoronically conceived as "potentiality itself"—in Agamben's thoroughly non-Aristotelian assertion of ontological nondistinction ("To set in-potentiality aside is not to destroy it but, on the contrary,

20. Agamben, *Homo Sacer*, p. 11.
21. Ibid., p. 37 *et passim*.

to fulfill it, to turn potentiality back upon itself in order to give itself to itself . . . letting itself be . . ."), the mystical or, at least, mystifying equation of politics to ontology that is *Homo Sacer*.[22]

For, it is Agamben's signature thesis that the history of "metaphysics" in general; the incomplete, because excessively relational, or, insufficiently absolutist, social theories of Foucault and Arendt in particular; and Benjamin, Kafka, and Hölderlin, in adhering to the textual tradition of the transmission of ungrounded linguistic convention in history, instead of dreaming an end to the history of philosophy *and* politics ("the 24 centuries that [since Aristotle] . . . have brought only provisional and ineffective solutions"), in a nonrelational ontology yet to be "invented," have all failed to conclude definitively, as has Agamben, that the "completely new politics" especially suited to "a new planetary order," modernity's supposedly singular proclivity, on this remarkably naïve view, for reducing human to bare life ("The Foucauldian thesis will then have to be corrected or, at least, completed, in the sense that what characterizes modern politics is not so much the inclusion of the *zoē* in the *polis* . . . [but that] exclusion and inclusion, outside and inside, *bios* and *zoē,* right and fact, enter into a zone of irreducible indistinction") is, more theocratically than theoretically speaking, a "politics beyond all figure of relation" (a nonstarter of a notion when it comes to understanding the political but a perfectly accurate description of the "potentiality" of a gun).[23] As far as concerns the "sovereign," the

22. Ibid., p. 46.

23. Ibid., pp. 11–12, 9, 47. See Catherine Mills' assessment that the "radical rejection of relationality" advocated by Agamben "appears to be premised on the elimination of alterity altogether" ("Playing with Law," p. 31). Mills importantly relates Agamben's explicit antipathy to relational thought, if not the possibility of thinking (in *Homo Sacer* and its reiterative companion works), his encomium of what he calls "immediate linguistic and ontological transparency" (*The Coming Community* [1993]) and the "beatitude" of "the happy life" (*Potentialities* [1999]), to his early attraction, in *Infancy and History* (*Infanza e historia* [1978]), to a nonlinguistic "unification of life" identified with "the originary experience of infancy, an experience that ontologically precedes and institutes the caesura of language and signification" (26, 33).

self-defining and all-deciding "power" said to *precede* "all figure of relation"—for Agamben the beginning and end (rather than suspension) of all reflection, the self-replicating mode effectively enacted in his own—even the possibility of drawing distinctions and relations between the human and nonhuman, between any activity and any other activity is, because it must be, leveled, evacuated, as a matter of fact: thus, the "exception" equates to the "rule," the "outside" to the "inside," "nature" to "law," "violence" to "justice," "animal life" to "human life," "democracy" to "totalitarianism," the technological prolongation of life without known consciousness by contemporary medicine to the technological extermination of conscious life by Nazism, so-called "potentiality" to so-called "non-potentiality," and finally, *as if*, *pace* the mortal indications of Lanzmann, *which side of the tracks you were standing on could have ever mattered in the slightest*, the "state," as such, equates to "the concentration camp."

That the response to depravity without limit, to the effort of total dehumanization in a place—to cite, with Agamben, Arendt—"where everything is possible," is the totalizing conceptualization *of* depravity as instead metaphysically necessary, the resurrection of an additionally reductive version of Hobbes's equation of the human to the bestial camouflaged, Trojan Horse–like, in a false analogy with everyday language and the excising exercise of erudition as of a sacerdotal authority—that one eventual outcome of the "modern" construction and demarcation of hell upon the earth would be the retrospective assertion, in a sampling of Roman legal prescriptions stitched to citation from current medical and legal literature, that all earth is hell, may be only one of the most aberrant consequences in recent history of overstepping history *and* the real demands of theory: the act of distinguishing "here" from "'here,'" which is to say, ontology from politics, a piece of earth from referent, dust from equally biodegradable human ashes.

Perhaps the most remarkable and theoretically honest consequence of Agamben's conceptual reification of genocide as "biopolitics" is his conclusion that the only alternative to the notion of mass murder as religious "sacrificial" orgy is the "truth" of Hitler's own categorization of the exterminated as "lice": "the truth—which it is difficult for the victims to face, but which we must have the courage not to cover with sacrificial veils—is that the Jews were exterminated not in a mad and giant holocaust but exactly as Hitler had announced, 'as lice,' which is to say, as bare life."[24] That it is another form of madness to reproach "the victims"—who are, by definition, dead—for failing to "face" this "truth" of their extermination goes without further comment. (Here Agamben makes the invocation of "truth" and "courage" in Heidegger's Freiburg *Rektoratsrede* welcoming the "challenge" of fascism appear but a conceptual misstep, the unfortunate mistaking of a certain man-made political reality for thinking. For Agamben the problem is rather the reverse: the transmillennial metaphysical mistake, or non-lice-like notion, of thinking any thinking can be distinguished from sovereign reality at all.) That the extermination of lice or any other form of "bare life" does not require the construction and maintenance of the camp—the walled, barbed-wire differentiation of "inside" and "outside"; the technology and orchestration of international deportation; the duplicity, secrecy, and demonstrated terror required for the mass murder of human beings alone—may indeed, however, need to be pointed out. The ways in which the individuals who die among individuals by mass murder, and the "survivors" who witness mass murder, and those active and complicit in mass murder, experience these events, can as little be known in any general, absolute, or exhaustive sense as that knowledge can be equated with that which it is not worth knowing, how "lice" meet their end. To consider such events the necessary outcome of "biopolitics" is to further finalize the final solution, equating, with the urgency of a theoretical solution, the view of their killer with what should be the true and acknowledged view of their killing by the victims. One requires only a passing acquaintance with human life, let alone with its commemoration and examination in literature and philosophy, to recognize the particularity onto infinity of each momentary part of the life of each finite human. Confirming the murder of a devised part of humanity as lice extermination instead only conceptually reinforces the reduction of the human to the state "beyond all figure of relation" at which Hitler

24. Agamben, *Homo Sacer*, p. 114.

indeed aimed, conflating the theoretical solution of the "problem" of the final solution with that solution itself.

Such "courageous" equations of "truth" with genocidal truisms as this one from *Homo Sacer*; the equally opportunistic assertions of truth-by-etymological-election with which Agamben replaces rather than analyzes discourse; and the sophistic conclusions exhibited in the still more simplistic *Remnants of Auschwitz: The Witness and the Archive*, in which the consistently scrupulous texts of Primo Levi are distorted in a declarative rhetoric conferring upon their author a second, conceptual death—*viz.*, now, "[Auschwitz] is everywhere," "in the normalcy of everyday life" (26); the "capacity" for the specifically "inhuman" is what was lacking in "the SS" (77)—have encouraged their own informal dismissal as evidence of old-fashioned "stupidity," a non-explanation doing a disservice to that conceptually complex term even as it conceals an old-fashioned, Christological, and specifically non-kabbalist, mysticism of the mind on Agamben's part, whose "coming community" of nondistinction, merely the other side of the coin equating metaphysics with totalitarianism, is that of an equally totalizing kingdom-come. As for the commonplace response, that such statements are so "stupid" as not to be taken seriously—the kind of reflex reaction of which one might think recent and not so recent history would have disabused us—it is precisely because of the imperviousness of real "stupidity" to the powerful seductions of a desired mystical transumption that one would do better to search in a *Dictionary of Received Ideas*, acknowledged *bêtises* like those assembled by Flaubert's Bouvard and Pécuchet, than in Agamben's *Remnants* for a definition of "Auschwitz."[25]

25. On the barely disguised re-enactment of the Christ story in Agamben's writings on "Auschwitz" (a re-enactment requiring, one should add, its own latter-day imitations of Paul, in the tautological distillation and enforcement of that story as source of personal political power by Agamben's disciples), and Agamben's own "unconscious" repetition of "the Nazis' gesture" in positing a notion of "reality absolutely separated from language" such as he purports to critique, see Dominick LaCapra, *History in Transit*, pp. 183–93, 171. On the basis of the politically opportunistic "effectivity" of papal power throughout its history, examined and exemplified in the writings of Agamben's model political theologian, Schmitt—that of a "paradigm" or "'principle of represen-

Finally, the most perceptive gloss on Agamben's, at best, mystical turn of mind, is provided by Kant. In the great, late essay, "Of a newly elevated, superior tone in philosophy" ("Von einem neuerdings erhobenen vornehmen Ton in der Philosophie" [*Berliner Monatsheft*, May 1796]), Kant, too, attempts to analyze "a certain mystical cadence, an overreaching jump (salto mortale) from concepts to the unthinkable" that, embraced in the wake of his own Critique, produced proponents of the kind of "mystical illumination" and "fanatical vision" that are "the death of all philosophy."[26] In the "clubbist" need of such self-appointed "mystagogues" for apostolic "adepts" ("in opposition to the people, understood as all the uninitiated") to whom they "speak" with a "godlike understanding" considered "superior" to the "discursive capacity for representation" and "capacity for thinking" on which "all understanding" depends, Kant further acknowledges the sociological consequences of these "monarchists out of envy, who now set Plato, and now, Aristotle, upon the throne . . . in the consciousness of their own inability to think [*Monarchisten aus Neid: die bald den Plato, bald den Aristotles auf den Thron erheben . . . bei dem Bewusstsein ihres eigenes Unvermögens, selbst zu denken*]."[27] An enduring admirer of (French) republican ideals in the years preceding their usurpation by imperial designs, Kant did not, however, foresee the abuse of human history, in addition to that of the human capacity for thinking, including the thinking of human equality, to which the "fatal leap" of such "mystagoge[ry]" might eventually extend.

tation'" subsuming all representation to the "representation of Christ on the cross"—see Sam Weber, "'The Principle of Representation,'" esp. pp. 30, 35–36.

26. Kant, *Werkausgabe*, VI: 387, A 406; 396, A 425.

27. Ibid., VI: 388, A 410; 389–90, A 412–13; 383, A 309.

4. Goethe after Lanzmann: Literature Represents "*X*"

LANZMANN'S "'inside'" and "'outside the camp'" refer to nonextant places that separated the living from the dead, and, as much as the eradication of architecture entails the eradication of the referent—not its necessary exclusion by way of linguistic systematization, nor its metaphoric and conceptual positing and transformation, but its material erasure, as if it is not and had never been—so architecture constitutes the referents, the grounds, to which historical life and language adhere. This study is not, like Lanzmann's great cinematic work, about methods of destruction applied in reality to affect the course of empirical history, methods engineered *not out of any empirical, physical necessity* but to make history itself conform at all costs to a certain *idea* of history. This real history of history enacted to embody an idea, and so destroy, as efficiently and rapidly as the practicalities of engineering such destruction allowed, as many bodies pertaining to a privative definition of spirit as could be found, is one whose own reality, however, continues to be brought into question, despite (or is it precisely in still lethal response to) the continuing efforts to retrieve, not those lost forever, but, rather, some knowledge of them, to link "who," across the abyss of how, with "where."[28]

28. Those efforts have recently been individualized in Daniel Mendelsohn's *The Lost: A Search for Six of the Six Million*, a work whose demonstrated tenacity of purpose and scrutiny of detail are reflected in the sinuousness, the unmuted self-reflexivity of its own prose style. In attending to the infinite quality of research as to that of any individual consciousness, Mendelsohn's project and its discursive record offer an at once modest ("six") and thus appropriately immodest ("of the six million") rejoinder to the absolutist negation of the particular experience of living, itself supposedly abstractable by sover-

The enormity of these efforts is only commensurate with the destruction they document. Yet, like "facts on the ground"—pieces of earth set aside for the purpose of transforming the arbitrariness of life into all-purpose, absolutely determined death—the indication ("'here'") of referents signified by the words ("'inside'" and "'outside'") that the separation of the multiform processes of living from repetitive, methodical murder requires, seems, as Lanzmann at once demonstrates and strives to prevent, always poised on the verge of disappearing. That the referent is necessary to history and occluded by history is the reality of history, and no fiction. In making the last turn in the course of a long study of the interrelationship of noncognitive, architectural form and literary and philosophical forms of discursive cognition, the current study finally approaches the referent and the reality of history through their representation in fiction.

For, in fiction, in which nothing is extant, Lanzmann's eerie insistence upon indicating a referent that, all-important historically, no longer exists, even as the earth that once bore its marks, and still bears the act of indicating, materially persists—in fiction, such a moment of pure reference is not the exception but the rule, the grounds upon which monuments to prevent historical oblivion are built. Goethe's marking of his own fictions by building—the construction, to fatal effect, of a "new" ground for "free human beings" to "stand on" in *Faust*, a drama whose "restless" action springs from the flat refusal of "dead" language and time; and the exposure, beneath a "free and open sky," of the "secret" "buried," like the dead, beneath all building, the "hidden ground" underlying the ubiquitous architectural activity preceding, accompanying, and succeeding the constitution of *Wahlverwandtschaften* throughout his novel—are literary entailments of the architectural that represent what Lanzmann's at once real and phantom "'here'" reveals: the coeval faces, or functions, of architectural activity viewed historically.

These are, on the one hand, the eradication, by way of buildings erected on the ground, of the very basis of life, the given vitality of

eign rule from life, whenever that negation is indicated as a (if not *the*) positive intellectual good under the deathly nomenclature, "biopolitics."

transient, destructible bodies, and, on the other, the founding, by building into the ground, of the referents of not any but specifically human life, of lives lived with language, in whatever sensuous form and through whatever system of cognitive signs language assumes. Just as the act of building eradicates natural life, life as given, while the matter of building serves to house and protect life, artificially prolonging it and its memory, so the eradication of buildings reveals material foundations, artificial grounds built into the earth, below the appearance of natural life, that may serve only as referents—and as such are the only referents—for possible historical knowledge. As opposed to the naturalization and conceptualization of the "referent," which is to say, its destruction *as* referent—whether by way of a supposed rejection or full embrace of language as identical with world, or through a wished-for suspension of all building by endless nomadic movement in space, and so of historical life by "life" that, neither historical nor natural, is never arrested at any moment in time, that comprehends no particular life, no particular death, speaks no language and leaves no trace—this book instead studies language together with the architectural, ultimately finding in their confluence, in Goethe's texts and in related formulations by Heidegger, by Benjamin, and by Kant, that which neither language nor building individually effects. It finds a founding of the referent in the conjunction of two materially different, inherently artificial forms, forms that, unlike birdsongs and beehives, have no basis, other than that imagined by desire or ideology, in nature.

Each internally articulated and externally malleable, intertwined with living and its memorialization, with sensory experience and its demise, language is never and building is always contingent upon a specific part of space, bound to a ground: a "'here'" that can never "take the place" of language inasmuch as language itself can only "take place" figuratively; a "'here'" that, just as unable to speak for itself, joins the word that takes no place to history.

PART I

Goethe's Timelessness

"to stand with a free people upon a free foundation"
["*auf freiem Grund mit freiem Volke stehn*"]

FAUST, in *Faust II*

1. Faust's Building: Theory as Practice

WITH THE EXCEPTION of the remarkable discussion of *Faust* by Marshall Berman, whose classic, still searing dialectical analysis of modernity as both constitutive and destructive of history, concluding with Robert Moses' devastation of the Bronx, departs from "the tragedy of development" defined for Berman in Goethe's play, scant if any critical notice has been made of the fact that, of all the acts of transgression Faust commits over the duration of his colorful drama, it is neither seduction, nor desertion, nor even murder that brings about his wager's loss.[1] The erotic "pull" of "the eternal feminine"

1. Berman, *All That Is Solid*, esp. pp. 60–86. In an essay devoted to the final scene of *Faust II*, and which itself opens, as if by way of analogy, with a discussion of textual study after Auschwitz, Adorno argues that the piecemeal quality of composition in *Faust II* derives from its necessary "forgetting" of Part I. While Adorno ultimately refers to Faust's intended founding of a "new ground" for mankind and consequent destruction of the cottage of Philemon and Baucis, he does not note the contradiction between Faust's exhaustive desire to redesign the world he sees, excepting no part or place in it from his plan, and the purported saving grace of the pointedly underschematized dramatic structure of Part II. Identifying Faust with Goethe on his deathbed and, perhaps, with Europe on its own, Adorno instead argues that Faust is saved because, by mere "force of living on" and "forgetting," he has changed: "Is not Faust saved because he is no longer at all he who signed the pact; does not the wisdom of the play in pieces lie in how little man is identical with himself . . . ? The force of life, as a living on, is equated with forgetting." (Adorno, "Zur Schlussszene dest Faust," p. 366).

While Adorno, at the time—and place—of the composition of the essay on *Faust II*, had every reason to engage in (uncharacteristic) wishful thinking regarding both the possibility of forgetting and its balming effect, there is no

and contrasting pastoral fealty of Philemon and Baucis may offer the most fertile ground for commentary on Faust's impassioned trajectory, but it is a decidedly impersonal act that brings the eventful course of his actions to an end. Sitting before the sea toward the close of *Faust II*, a world-weary Mephisto at his side, Faust regards natural phenomena—here, the repetitive "play" of the advancing waves ("With time the play repeats itself" [*Die Stunde kommt, sie wiederholt das Spiel*] [*Faust II*, IV.10209])—with the same contemptuous impatience he had reserved for verbal phenomena in *Faust I*. The thrust of Faust's final complaint reflects and reverses his first and, in that inverted symmetry, the arc of development spanning both plays first appears revealed. For, standing with Wagner before the city gate at the opening of *Faust I*, the disgruntled scholar had described as "a beautiful dream" the natural scene he now rejects: "I rush to drink the [goddess's] eternal light, / Before me the day and behind me the night, / The sky above me and under me the waves. / A beautiful dream" [*Ich eile fort, ihr ew'ges Licht zu trinken, / Vor mir den Tag und hinter mir die Nacht, / Den Himmel über mir und unter mir die Wellen. / Ein schöner Traum*] (*Faust I*, 1086–89). "Waves" rolling "below" him, and "the sky above," it is no longer the uselessness of human learning and knowledge that inspires Faust's anger ("Precisely what

evidence, but rather a life's works of counterevidence (*Die Wahlverwandtschaften* first among these), that Goethe viewed oblivion as anything but a visually induced state of aberrancy, a temporary absence of mind issuing in unsuspected and permanent concrete loss.

In *Goethes Faust*, Peter Brandes endorses what he characterizes as Adorno's view of forgetting as the "power of transformation," and traces such a concept of forgetting taking place "beyond the economy of guilt" from Nietzsche through Kommerell, Adorno, and Derrida: "Faust has become another not through his becoming as striving but through his forgetting, whereby his forgetting is hardly to be designated his own, but is rather the gift, the gift of forgetting" (200–204). Although Brandes recognizes that Derrida's conception of "radical forgetting" includes its own contradiction of oblivion in the trace, and uses Derrida's notion of trace to discuss the anticipatory articulation of the *Augenblick* that precipitates Faust's death, he maintains an uneasy identity of forgetting with "future-oriented" remembering, of the kind: "The forgetting of forgetting is itself a remembering of the possibility of this form of forgetting" (203–4).

we don't know, is what we could use / And what we do know, is of no use" [*Was man nicht weiss, das eben brauchte man, / Und was man weiss, kann man nicht brauchen*] [*Faust I*, 1066–67]) in *Faust II*, but rather nature's inhuman lack of vision and ambition, the "purposeless power of unbound elements" [*zwecklose Kraft unbändiger Elemente*], "wave conquering wave . . . and nothing accomplished" [*Da herrschet Well' auf Welle . . . und es ist nichts geleistet*] (*Faust II*, IV.10216–17).

Just as Faust's earlier idealization of the pure dynamism of nature has turned in time to disenchantment with its "purposeless power," so the very mental faculties he had once discounted as impotent now inspire him. Recognizing his separateness from nature as the positive source of an unnatural power—the intertwined abilities to analyze and act upon the "given" relations of force in nature rather than give oneself to them,[2] Faust "swiftly forms plans" [*Da fasst' ich schnell im Geiste Plan auf Plan*] (*Faust II*, IV.10227) to do for nature what she cannot do for herself. He will now divert, store and distribute the undirected "streams" of energy he "strove" to experience immediately in *Faust I* (1676, 1720, 1742) so as to arrive, by means of those natural energies, at an entirely artificial end, a monument not to nature's powers but to man's supernatural ability to turn them about,

2. "Let us crash into the rush of time, / Into the rolling round of givenness" [*Stürzen wir uns in das Rauschen der Zeit, / Ins Rollen der Begebenheit*] (Faust I, 1754–55). As the present analysis develops, the consciousness of time underpinning Faust's desire in *Faust I*—his view that, by hurling himself into the natural course of things, he will in effect embrace time *per se*, thus eluding all experience of specific temporal change—is no less determinative of the architectonic project, proceeding from a directly opposite approach to "givenness," that he oversees in *Faust II*.

One of the best studies of *Faust* to date, Jane K. Brown's *Goethe's Faust*, provides a welcome, in-depth analysis of the "nonmimetic" structure and content of the play, the "nonillusionist, "allegorical," and "operatic" mode whose anti-Aristotelian dramatic models are "world literature" and the world-as-play literature of Calderón and Shakespeare, and whose philosophical and literary antecedents are to be found in Milton, Goldsmith, Rousseau, Gay, and Rowe, rather than a fledgling Germanic tradition (21, 35, 149, 208ff, *et passim*). See the continuation of this note in the Appendix.

to yield a certain independent end by intervening in and altering the continuum of cause and effect. Faust's plans would submit "the unbound elements" of nature to new operations and configurations, funneling the formless dynamism of tidal waters into mechanically sealed containers—canals for shipping—and forming matter by building dams to retrieve ocean breakfront for useable land. Rejecting the instability of the natural power he sees before him, a power always in the course of moving on, negating at every moment its own visible formations, Faust would now coerce substance from force, form from movement, extant ground from what "is" not.

Always violent in their proposals, husbanders of nature never come bidden. By turns persuasive and despotic, they ply, undermine, compel: their plans, viewed without measure as the material realization of reason itself, mean to subordinate whatever or, by the same token, whomever it is that "stands" in their way. Having performed the roles of husband and progenitor on the small and large stage with Gretchen and Helen, Faust now turns from all mimetic and allegorical theater of action to an inimitable scene and its creation, a project, rather than play, of inhuman scope: the reworking of the physical contours and qualities of the given world itself. The dream of experiencing nature as if part of nature's own flowing, motive force ("to flow through nature's veins" [*durch die Adern der Natur zu fliessen*] [*Faust I*, 619]), of being one with the very energy of infinite change ("only restless activity truly occupies man" [*nur rastlos betätigt sich der Mann*] [*Faust I*, 1759]), is replaced by the opposing dream of imposing permanent change through external means, of transforming nature's fluidity into enclosed liquid masses, and ebbing, visible surfaces into durable solids. Faust's final act on earth is just that: the founding of a new ground, or ungrounded foundation, upon the earth itself. His "land-reclamation" project does not truly aim to reclaim, nor even to replace or resituate. It would instead establish, out of natural repetitive movement and displacement, their opposite: *a place which is an origin, an origin which is a place.*[3]

3. In his 1928 essay on Goethe in *Die literarische Welt*, Benjamin describes Faust's "reclaiming of land from the sea" as "an activity which nature prescribes to history and in which nature is itself inscribed—that was Goethe's conception of historical action" (Benjamin, *Gesammelte Schriften*, II:739). Now,

Thus Faust's original desire, for the immediate, contingent experience of sensuous reality, becomes the will to construct the independent basis for all such experience, an origin anterior to the origin of desire, an absolutely necessary or noncontingent place.[4] Faust attempts to achieve on and by means of the earth what Plato's interlocutors, unable to define justice in terms of individual experience and perception, are led by his Socrates to view on the nonanalogous model of the state. Socrates' disingenuous comparison of the individual and the organized city as equivalent embodiments of justice distinct merely in scale (or, to recall Socrates' graphic metaphor, as a single text written in "small" and "large letters") replaces the irresolvable problem of *knowing* just human practice with an organized *fiction* precluding epistemological quandaries: a purely theoretical

---

while it is certainly true that Goethe identified history and natural history as a single active and cognitive domain, it is not at all true that we may identify Goethe with Faust, no more than it is to assert that it is nature that "prescribes to history" its own undoing in Faust's land-reclamation project. On the contrary, it is precisely its equal opposition to nature and history that defines Faust's project and, with it, both the peripeteia and dénouement of his drama, as his building of an origin without precedent, a place free from both natural and historical "prescription" (in Benjamin's terms), results ultimately in the expressed wish that this origin *as* origin linger and so constitute its own natural history, a joining of unmitigated beauty to duration that defines not his design but, quite the contrary, his bet.

4. By contrast, Eric Blackhall, even while emphasizing that Faust's final "concern is . . . with the earth and man's place upon it," describes "the project of reclaiming land from the sea" as psychologically motivated: "satisf[ying] [Faust's] desire for power, control and dominion" (see Blackhall, *Faust's Last Speech*, p. 5). Similarly, while noting the explicitly external, "topographical" language of Faust's final speech, Blackhall interprets that language as "symbolic" of an internal, all too human struggle: "Faust's vision is topographical, but it can also be interpreted symbolically, with the phrase 'im Innern hier' referring not just to the polderlands but to the mind of man, constantly assailed from without as are the polderlands" (7). Blackhall had already characterized the external aspect of Faust's project positively even with regard to the very people, places and earth it supplants; Faust's "vision," he writes "involves not just personal dominion but heritage to others, and not just colonization but preservation against the eroding forces—of nature!" (6).

polis whose machine-like workings exclude, precisely, the human element, the ability "to imitate all things" [*mimeisthai panta chremata*] personified by, but not limited to, the poets explicitly banished in *Republic*, Bk. III.[5] Just as Socrates' new city, according to Socrates' prescriptive theory, will remain free from contingency as long as its constituent elements maintain their prescribed relations, neither transgressing nor exchanging their particular formal functions (*erga*), so Faust's constitution, from newly configured elements, of an original or fully independent, concrete place doubles as the project for a polis ontologically prior to the need for speculative political theory. Faust's "plans" give rise to a basis for human activity that, from the outset, need never reflect on acting justly, for this is a basis or ground as independent of natural change as it is of human history. It is thus, in the most forceful (and anti-social) sense of those terms, a new or "free ground" for "a free people to stand on" [*auf freiem Grund mit freiem Volke stehn*] (*Faust II*, V.11580), a people literally, empirically set apart from the consequential, if often ontologically ungrounded events historical life entails: a people as free of those chains of historical steps and missteps as it is dependent, in its own existence, on the construction of a previously nonexistent ground.

Like Plato's philosopher-king compelled from a cave of illusory shadow-play to stand in and see the light of the sun, Faust conceives

5. Plato, *Republic*, II.368d–369b3; III.398a. The famous critique of the unfettered mimetic arts of epic, tragedy, and comedy, and resultant argument for censoring or banishing poets for the good of a hypothetical, purely functionalist state, occupies the first half of Bk III (III.386–398c), and informs, often in pointedly non-hypothetical terms, the ongoing tradition of "platonic" literary and art criticism in the west, itself tending to bifurcate, revealingly if inevitably, along frequently incompatible "aesthetic" and "moral" lines. I have previously discussed the illogical premise on which the *Republic*, both dialogue and city, are grounded—Socrates' originary detour from defining "the justice of one man" [*dikaiosyne . . . esti men andros enos*] to that attributed to "an entire city" [*esti de pou kai oles poleos*], and thus to a delineation not of "the force proper . . . of the greatest human good" [*te autou dynamei . . . dikaiosyne de megiston agathon* (II.366e7–367a1)] but of the predefined, pointedly mechanistic functioning of a nonhuman, architectonic state—in "Architecture in the Discourse of Modern Philosophy," esp. 19–21.

of a place made by force from which the Good may finally be perceived, for, of all the forms of "the intelligible world"—so Plato's Socrates—"the Good is the last to be seen."[6] But whereas Socrates makes clear he considers practice inferior to theory as a means of grasping the true reality of intelligible forms, and that his conception of the well-functioning city may instruct us about justice exactly because it is a theoretical conception, "formulated in words" rather than "realize[d] . . . in practice," Faust demands the complete and immediate identity of thought and action, theory and practice.[7] If, for Plato's Socrates, the true measure of "things . . . described in theory" is never and can never be whether they "exist precisely in practice," for Goethe's Faust *there is and can be no theory*, properly speaking: there is and there can only be realization, *and that realization must itself be material.*[8] That is to say, it must be built: structural rather than individual, hard rather than human, a thing of substance rather than either mimesis or speculation. Faust's "newest world" [*neust(e) Erde* (*Faust II*, V.11566)], like Plato's theoretical state, establishes an origin in architectonic form, the one extracted from physical matter, the other "formulated in words." Yet for Faust to see his construction project realized, actually to see the origin of what was not before—a new time embodied in the founding of a new earth—his architectonic design must be put into practice, must be made earthly architecture, *now*: construction must reflect conception as if its own simultaneous mirror image. For in the passage of time between the design and realization, the thinking and building, of a thing, the architectonic moment of its origin is lost, or, rather, loses its identity: once reflected upon, that conceptual moment is doubled, re-enacted, repeated differently in time. This elision of the new into the old, of an architectonic vision into the painstaking making of

6. Plato, *Republic*, VII.517b8–c1: "*en to gnosto teleutaia e tou agathou idea kai mogis orasthai.*"

7. Plato, *Republic*, V.473a1–2: "*e physin egei praxin legeos etton aletheias ephaptesthai.*"

8. Plato, *Republic*, V.473a5–6: "*to logo dielthomen, toiauta pantapasi kai to ergo dien gignomena apophainein.*" See V.473a–b2 for Socrates' full discussion and distinction of the incommensurate truth values of theory and practice.

architected matter, is precisely what Faust strives to avoid. Speed and immediacy are the inherently violent requirements for the forced subordination of architecture to architectonics:

> What I have thought, I rush to realize;
> Only the word of the master has weight.
> Up from your camps, you slaves! Man for man!
> Let that which I boldly conceived be seen!
> Grab the tools! Stir shovel and spade!
> What has been staked out must immediately come to pass.
> On strict orders, rash industry
> Wins the loveliest prize;
> For the greatest work to be realized
> A thousand hands need but one mind.
>
> [*Was ich gedacht, ich eil' es zu vollbringen;*
> *Des Herren Wort, es gibt allein Gewicht.*
> *Von Lager auf, ihr Knechte! Mann für Mann!*
> *Lasst glücklich schauen, was ich kühn ersann!*
> *Ergreift das Werkzeug! Schaufel rührt und Spaten!*
> *Das Abgesteckte muss sogleich geraten.*
> *Auf strenges Ordnen, raschen Fleiss*
> *Erfolgt der allerschönste Preis*
> *Dass sich das grösste Werk vollende,*
> *Genügt ein Geist für tausend Hände*] (*Faust II*, V.11501–11510)

Having "conceived" of a "work" whose design is itself a conception of matter, a work producing not a particular building but a general ground or foundation for building, Faust's is the ruling "mind" for which "a thousand hands" labor in synch, and these synecdochic movers of matter are not only mindless and faceless, but bodiless. Enslaved to the "shovel and spade" they animate, the final conduits of an internal physical power they supply, these "hands" are nothing in themselves but bunches of expendable digits, rudimentary means, akin to their arithmetic namesakes, for performing another's will. Faust's conception of the "ground" for "a free people" yields a violently instrumentalist ("*Ergreift das Wekzeug!*"), thoroughly dehumanizing practice because this "master"-builder acts at once as

Socrates and Socrates' hypothesized philosopher-king. His own is the "mind," which envisions a new earth *and* oversees its realization.[9]

Such an identification of theory with practice, idealized in theory, proves worse than murderous in practice. For, in striving to supplant the temporal difference between the two—"Let that which I boldly *conceived* be *seen*"—Faust's attempt to render theory "immediately" material must exploit an assembled labor force in a manner unbefitting animals. Extracting energy at all hours and in absolute disregard for the life of its individual repositories, Faust neither intends nor, what is worse, conceives the change that the prosecution of his project imposes upon the corporal economy of the exploitation of labor. For the immediacy of result required by Faust's labor project excludes from its execution even the minimal rational requirement of maintaining the life of the enslaved, favoring in the stead of the rational, a pure consumption of labor, one that effectively supplants labor (the real product alienated from a subject and converted into exchange value by an economy geared instead toward capital accumulation) with the fundamentally anti-economic principle of pure work (lacking a subject of alienation and medium of accumulation

9. Comparing the ending of *Faust II* with Balzac's contemporaneously written *Peau de chagrin* (in *Faust und Faustus*, p. 128), Lukács employs metaphors of flooded land to contrast Balzac's "modern" creation of "a new epic form" out of the "ripping apart of the dams of the old forms by the storm flood" of capitalism, with Goethe's "regulation of the water current through old, newly imaged forms." Without noting that Faust's enforced labor project aims precisely at the actual, physical creation of "new ground" from floodland, Lukács coincidentally gives voice to the modernity of Faust's, if not his author's project, as well as to the material consequences of striving for "formal completion" in the shaping of earthly, rather than social or literary, "power lines":

> In Balzac: fantastic prelude to the modern novel, in which the at once real and phantomlike quality of capitalistic life comes to expression. In Goethe: fantastic final agreement of the last period of complete form in bourgeois literature. Balzac and Goethe both experience this brimming over of new life, the ripping apart of the dams of the old forms by the storm flood. But Balzac seeks to ground the inner power lines of this spilling over, in order to allow a new epic form to arise out of their recognition; Goethe undertakes a regulation of the current through old, newly imaged forms.

whatsoever), which is to say, work which equates to absolute corporal expenditure, work unto death. Individuals die but not so the force of work, which, as the pure, abstract form of labor, provides Faust with an operational concept free from human referents, a self-defining idea as noncontingent as the concrete place Faust would have such force make.[10]

10. Neither epistemological nor allegorical in its fundamental identity and function, Faust's final act of building, concretely different from all his other acts, is, I think, mischaracterized by Brown as a coequal part of the artificial tradition of internal creativity she so ably discusses throughout her study:

> In Act III, Faust created Arcadia "in play"; we recognized this as an artistic act. Now [Faust] creates his Arcadia in the world. To the extent that both temporarily impose a vision on the raw stuff of nature, they are the same . . . Creation is the act that turns the moment into the highest moment out of time, the act that validates human existence. But it is, as Act I had explicitly shown, something that comes from within . . . [Mephisto] cannot be expected to speak directly for the creative power, the life force that we have been calling spirit. As the embodiment of world he is more accurate when he says 'Time triumphs' (I. 11592) for the ultimate triumph of time is Faust's recognition that every single moment can be a moment of revelation" (Brown, *Goethe's Faust*, 239–40).

Similar to Brown's view of Faust's "creativity," while taking, unlike Brown, a morally transcendent view of such art, is Neil Flax's conclusion that

> the culmination of Faust's long education in Mephistopheles's school of art is that he finally transforms himself into an artist, a creator, a conjurer of new worlds out of a compound of his own commanding words, Mephistopheles's demonic magic, and the material reality of nature. To be sure, his creation of a new paradise on earth is a self-delusion, but all art, as the play has repeatedly shown, is delusion. The important point is that Faust, as a creator, has finally tapped into the divine sources of being and is thus ready to ascend to a higher realm. (See Flax, "Goethe and Romanticism," p. 46.).

Günther Mieth, by contrast, commends Goethe's refusal, in Faust's reiteration of the historical consciousness banned in his wager, "to sublate historical development and dialectic in a utopia," whether of "creative" or theoretical origin (see Mieth, "Fausts letzter Monolog" p. 102).

A theory that conceives of itself as a praxis requires pure, universally applicable force, not limited, cognitive particulars, and in order to perform its identity with praxis it proceeds *per force*, with haste. The product it yields must appear unprecedented even by conception if that product, while thoroughly artificial, is nonetheless to be viewed as entirely self-identical: as a replacement of pre-existing natural relations that seems instead to pre-date *rather than* replace these. The ordered removal and consequent, if unplanned, murder of Philemon and Baucis—Faust to Mephistopheles: "So go and get rid of them [literally: "put them aside"]!" [*So geht und schafft sie mir zur Seite!*] (*Faust II*, V.11275)—recalls and revises, now as wholly innocent of sensory entrapment and seduction, the deathly consequences of Gretchen's plight in *Faust I*: the condemnation of provincial individuals in the context of a building project is specifically *not* the by-product of corporeal desire satisfied and spent. It is rather violence committed with a view to aesthetic absolutism, Faust's stated desire to "see" and "oversee" "all [he] has done" from a single, dominating perspective, i.e., "in one view" ("To see, all that I have done / To oversee with one glance / the masterpiece of the human spirit" [*Zu sehn, was alles ich getan, / Zu überschaun mit einem Blick / Des Menschengeistes Meisterstück*], [*Faust II*, V.11246–48]), that motivates the destruction of the aged couple.[11] As discussed later in this study, the

11. Cf. Heinz Hamm's pertinent observation, in "Julirevolution, Saint-Simonismus und Goethes Abschliessende Arbeit am *Faust*," that no practical, economic "necessity" but rather exclusively aesthetic demands determine Faust's elimination of Philemon and Baucis: "He would like to rest under the lindens alone and unbothered; and he would like finally to erect a look-out point upon them from which he can oversee his realm . . . Must the world of Philemon and Baucis be destroyed ["'hin' (V.11337) sein"] with the victory of Faust? In that he offers no compelling economic reason for the extermination of this world, Goethe did not intend us to see it as unpreventable" (90–91). Hamm here takes aim at Thomas Metscher's thesis in "*Faust* und die Ökonomie" that the play carries forth the historical and social development of the worker class, an argument that proleptically (and without self-irony) envisions a society freed from class struggle in Goethe's representation of slave labor. The necessarily architectural mode of achieving aesthetic sufficiency, as well as the independence from all historical necessity such an achievement would entail, are not however, noted by Hamm. In "Goethe's *Faust* Today," Hans

introduction and "setting aside" of the importunely located "Philemon" and "Baucis" present a perfectly complementary inversion of Goethe's historically precedent use of these conventional pastoral names: "Philemon, with his Baucis" first appear in *Die Wahlverwandtschaften* (Chapter One of Part Two), as the narrator describes the pleasant, purely visual effect of Charlotte's removal of all evidence of the location of the dead from the community graveyard.[12]

In direct contrast to their mention in Goethe's novel, in *Faust II* the classically derived Philemon and Baucis represent not complaisant spectators of, but temporal obstacles to the completion of a fully self-present or exclusively aesthetic "masterwork." Like their common history and residence in a "space" defined only by the presence of "linden trees" [*Lindenraum*], embodiments of nature that, while similarly classical in origin, are also equally visually obstructive—Faust: "My high estate, it is not pure / The linden-space with the brown built thing / and decaying little church is not mine" [*Der Lindenraum, die braune Baute, / Das morsche Kirchlein ist nicht mein*] (*Faust II*, V.11156–8)—the shared death of Philemon and Baucis,

---

Rudolf Vaget presents a definitive critique of all justification for Faust's final actions that bases itself on the Saint-Simonian notion of human "perfectibility" and the "social and political engineering" which it sanctions: "To an unbiased mind, there is no way to morally justify the expropriation of their property and the death of Philemon and Baucis . . . Faust's inspired vision [of a free people]—the C-Major fanfare trumpeted by all Marxist readings of *Faust*—is about as trustworthy as the vow of sobriety of a derelict alcoholic . . . Faust's last speech, all orthodox claims to the contrary, marks no conversion in a moral or political sense; it still bears the imprint of an authoritarian, power-hungry mind" (see Vaget, in *Interpreting Goethe's Faust Today*, pp. 53–54).

12. See, Goethe, *Werke*, VI: 361. For Goethe's explanation to Eckermann of his use of these "ancient" names, borrowed from Ovid, in *Faust II*—his serene disavowal that their appearance in the play was related in any way to their opposing fate in *Metamorphoses* Bk. 8, in which, in the tale told by Lelex, the gods instead reward Philemon and Baucis for their hospitality with a magnificent palace raised safely above floodwaters upon an island—and for an analysis of the relation between their removal in the play and the earlier "setting aside" of gravestones in the novel, see this study, Part Two, section 4, "Superfluous Stones," pp. 104–6.

and grisly report of their incineration alongside linden trees set aflame (*Faust II*, V.11304–35), confirm the cost exacted upon both historical nature and humanity by the perfection and completion of any pre-determined master plan. Yet Faust's plan would found a "new" context that could also, and *at the same time*, found the "free ground" from which that context can be "viewed" *in its totality*, as if ground and ocular field could ever be rendered entirely co-extensive, with or without the removal of any one and any place that interrupted, and so called into question, their visual identity.[13]

Just as it must violently remove the discretely visible from its constructed "new earth" and visual field, so it is that in Faust's conflation of them, theory-in-practice must, in effect, replace "re-place-ment," using the mode of substitution to erase its traces by imposing upon pre-existing relations a singular place, effacing from the act of replacement all persistent marks of diachrony as if sundering prefix ("re-") and suffix ("-ment") from the word that contains them. Space must be placed where these marks had been before, but in order for such space, and the new "place" it delimits, to present no grounds

13. It may well be precisely the persistent and recognizable historical humanity represented by "that old pair" [*jenes alte Paar*] (*Faust II*, V.11347), reflected in their evocation as "good old folk" [*die guten alten Leute*] (*Faust II*, V.11316) even by the eventual agent and messenger of their destruction, that has also made Philemon, Baucis, and their demise a preferred traditional measure for interpreting the inevitability of Faust's own rise and fall. Goethe's treatment of the "pair" within the play contrasts sharply with Faust's stated enslavement of a "thousand" working "hands," who, or which, are not only presented as entirely anonymous and without history but as nearly incorporeal, their bodily reality, not to speak of humanity, identified only in the reported perception, by Baucis, of "tortured cries" (*Faust II*, V.11128).

The radical depersonalization of Faust's labor force in Goethe's text extends to its critics, who have neglected to reflect upon this faceless crew, while lamenting the death of Philemon and Baucis, with remarkable consistency. Among the most prominent of these are Lukács (*Faust und Faustus*, p. 178); Erich Trunz ("Nachwort zu *Faust*," III:479), and Adorno ("Zur Schlussszene des Faust," pp. 336–37); preceding them, Paul Stöcklein (*Wege zum späten Goethe*, p. 88); and, more recently, Berman (*All that Is Solid*). See the continuation of this note in the Appendix.

for comparisons with places past, this replacement of one locus by another must also effect a necessary temporal contortion.[14] In suppressing the distinction, made only in the mind, between what was before and what came after, the act of replacement must appear to take place even *before* memory can be fully formed, that is, before the mind can recall the difference between "before" and "after" to the eye. Forcing disembodied "hands" to alter the earth overnight—"Pick and shovel, blow upon blow . . . There a dam on the next day stood" [*Hack' und Schaufel, Schlag um Schlag . . . Stand ein Damm den andern Tag*] (*Faust II*, V.11124–26); "The night rang with the cry of pain . . . In the morning it was a canal" [*Nachts erscholl des Jammers Qual . . . Morgens war es ein Kanal*] (*Faust II*, V.11128–30)—Faust aims to have produced a work that was never a work-in-progress. Completed under cloak of darkness, the rapid work of "pick and shovel" precludes the work of memory, making the resultant structure appear, like Socrates' Good, a fact as self-evident as the light of

14. In a monograph on his, Gide's, and Benjamin's travels to Moscow, Derrida offers a closely related perception of the singularly nonreferential status of the proper noun "U.S.S.R.," the only name given exclusively to a "state" rather than a particular place or national history: "the name of U.S.S.R. itself is the only name of a state in the world that carries with it no reference to a locality or a nationality. The only proper name of a state which finally carries with it no given proper noun, in the current meaning of the term: the U.S.S.R. is the only name of an individual as state [*individu étatique*], of an individual and singular State [*un État individual et singulier*], which gave to itself or intended to give to itself its own proper name [*son propre nom propre*] without reference to any singular place or any national past" (Jacques Derrida, *Moscou aller-retour*, p.17). The temporal complications inherent in such a nonreferential, "purely artificial, technical, conceptual" (18) self-naming are not considered explicitly at this moment by Derrida, nor, in a sense, need they be by us, since the "U.S.S.R.," name of an entity without reference to specific pre-existing place or history, to which Derrida traveled, as he states, "at the moment when certain Republics of the U.S.S.R. have begun to claim their independence," is itself no longer any but an *historical* name whose continuingly non-concrete reference is now instead to the very period of time during which its nonreferentiality functioned: the name of a state, referring to no specific place or national history, that has itself been historicized; the wholly "technical" name, that of an idea, now itself made into a thing of the past.

day by which it is seen. If the contrasting brutality of Faust's building project is the condition of its rapid, non-Socratic realization of theory in practice, the specific form in which that project makes its intellectual origin "immediately" material is, no less than that of the theoretical Platonic polis, architectonic.

Still, Socrates' replacement of the definition of individual human justice by a general fiction of mechanical *justesse*, a theoretical state of individuals reduced to single interlocking, inexchangeable functions, appears a mere verbal sleight-of-hand compared to Faust's violent isolation and impressing of "hands" into hard labor, for which, appropriately enough, there appears no classical precedent.[15] Indeed, compared to Faust's characteristically modern project of founding "a free people" on the invisible backs of enslaved laborers, even the

15. Nor does there appear to be any preceding reflection, in the critical literature, on Faust's reduction of enslaved laborers to disposable *Werkzeuge*. Neither Lukács, nor more recent Marxist criticism of the play by Thomas Zabka (see Zabka, *Faust II*), presents Faust's absolute expenditure and transformation of bodies into pure workforce as anything but an expression of the bourgeois tenet of "free" markets, even if Zabka sees, without additionally recognizing the contradiction of the market principle which his observation implies, that in Faust, "the idea of the free exchange becomes the reality of naked violence" (Zabka, 252). Lukács goes so far as to interpret Faust's brutal establishment of "new ground" as an expression of communal struggle, the "highest aim of humankind"; whereas, "like Goethe," Faust is "the opponent of all revolution," Lukács observes, "here, however, he . . . comes for the first time in his striving to the highest aim of humankind, which until now he had realized only in his personal development . . . to fight together with his fellow men" (Lukács, *Faust und Faustus*, p. 177). When Lukács does acknowledge "the gruesome rhythm of extermination that accompanies and comments on Faust's dream of the future," he assimilates that violence to the "adequate expression," by Goethe, of the "insolubility of the dissonance" of "capitalist development" (178). Berman, surprisingly, takes an even more romantic view, concluding that, for the witness to the "'blood shed'" by Faust's "'human sacrifices'" and the nightly "'tortured screams'" succeeded by the appearance of dams and canals in daylight, "there is something miraculous and magical about all this"; and adding that, as the overseer of slave laborers, Faust (much like any "vision"-driven C.E.O., or so conventional corporate rationale insists) is just as tough—although it is not clear how—on number one: "if he drives his workers hard, so he drives himself" (Berman, *All that is Solid*, pp. 64–65).

imperial design of the ancient gods, forcing a mourning prince to found Latinium, seems mild. The usurpation and pitiless slaying of noble Turnus, with whose bitter, dying glance the *Aeneid* abruptly concludes, can be interpreted as a pure consequence of force or fate depending on one's view of the "character" of his killer, the political or literary intentions of his decidedly post-Homeric author, or the late myth of the divine origin of Roman empire represented—at best ambivalently—in Virgil's poem. By contrast, Faust's ambition to *construct* a new ground is as anti-mythological as it is impersonal: from the outset it both is and is not his own. The wish to usurp the empire of nature itself has made the question of human *or* divine rule irrelevant for Faust (much as the blood sport of her own usurpation, the war of human empires, did for Helen). Architectural, rather than sexual or imperial, from the ground up—a "ground" which, in addition, it itself creates—this is an ambition for origin founded in the eradication of all natural and human conditions. Unlike Faust's early erotic drives, or any corporal impulse—actual, remembered, or imagined—this desire to build an original place renders the subject or subjects in whom it originates entirely immaterial. The ultimate aim of Faust's ambition is not to be one with the "body" of nature—indeed not to be, let alone unite with, any sensuous object at all—but to *extract force from that objective body, transfer and store it.*

Already referring to his own "earthly days" as a "trace" (*Faust II*, V.11583), Faust yearns not for more life but to relieve life of its sensory immediacy, to transpose animacy itself into a kind of holding pattern or script. While revealing, through the violence of its installation, a ground previously unexposed, the appearance of a delimited place where fluidity had naturally reigned, such a system of containment and translation destroys life as we know it, disassociating life from the living rather than ensuring the continuity of any being or beings, individual biology, growing empire, or group myth. Engendered mechanically, which is to say, concretely *and* abstractly, with force forcefully separated from its particular incorporation in order to be made available for universal application, this is a housing of energy as such in which Faust will not reside; indeed, its very construction anticipates his demise.

2. Faust's and Heidegger's Technology: Building as *Poiesis*

THE IMPERSONALITY of Faust's final goal is most adequately described not by Mephisto, whose representation of Faust's discontent extends only to the latter's sensuous desires ("No pleasure sates him, no happiness is enough" [*Ihn sättigt keine Lust, ihm gnügt kein Glück*] [*Faust II*, V.11587]), but by the later observations of a philosopher who does not appear to have had *Faust*, among Goethe's works, in mind. In his unsurpassed analysis of the "challenge" to nature and people posed by "modern technology," the replacement of natural historical relations with new "built-in" norms, Heidegger reveals the aim and lure of Faust's building project at its core. Technology, the material interruption and transformation of organic, or self-regulating, physical processes, permits the energy naturally expended by those processes to be extracted, contained, channeled, stored. Heidegger states and responds to the question posed by technology as follows:

> What is modern technology? It too is a revealing. . . .
>
> The revealing that rules in modern technology is a challenging, which puts to nature the unreasonable demand that it supply energy which can be extracted and stored as such. But does this not hold true for the old windmill as well? No. Its sails do indeed turn in the wind; they are left entirely to the wind's blowing. But the windmill does not unlock energy from the air currents in order to store it. . . .
>
> The hydroelectric plant is set into the current of the Rhine. It sets the Rhine to supplying its hydraulic pressure, which then sets the turbines turning; this turning sets those machines in motion

whose thrust sets going the electric current for which the long-distance power station and its network of cables are set up to convey electricity. In the realm of the interlocking processes pertaining to the ordering up of electrical energy, the current of the Rhine also appears as something ordered up. The electric plant is not built into the Rhine River like the old wooden bridge that joined bank with bank for hundreds of years. Rather, the river is built up into the power plant. What the river is as current now, namely, a water-power supplier, derives from the essence of the power station. . . .

The revealing that rules throughout modern technology has the character of a posing, in the sense of posing a challenge. Such challenging happens in that the energy concealed in nature is unlocked, the unlocked is transformed, the transformed is stored up, the stored up, in turn, is distributed, and the distributed is switched around anew. Unlocking, transforming, storing, distributing, and switching around are ways of revealing . . .

Who carries out the challenging posing through which what we call the real is revealed as standing reserve? Evidently man. To what extent is man capable of such a revealing? Man can, indeed, conceive, form, and carry out this or that in one way or another. Yet man does not have control over unconcealment itself, in which, from time to time, the real shows itself or withdraws.[16]

16. Heidegger, "Die Frage nach der Technik" [The Question Concerning Technology], pp. 14–17. For the original German, see the continuation of this note in the Appendix.

Although no reference is made to *Faust* in this watershed essay, which, in keeping with Heidegger's writing on material things in relation to Being, contemplates particular objects or constructs rather than invoking mythical or literary narratives in its analysis, Heidegger does explicitly cite, and importantly incorporate, in "Die Frage" a neologism from the *Wahlverwandtschaften.* Treating Goethe's language much as he would Parmenides', Heidegger highlights Goethe's introduction, in the "Novelle" within the novel, of the "mysterious word" [*geheimnisvolle Wort*], "*fortgewähre*'" (roughly, "to grant permanently") used instead of the customary "*fortwähren*" (to endure permanently). Heidegger proceeds to include the inserted particle of Goethe's new term in his own novel designation of the enduring essence of technology, "*Ge-*

What does it mean to remove energy from its material source, transform it into a new medium that can be channeled at will, hold it *ab situ*, and implement it in the execution of action with which it would otherwise have nothing to do? Technology, the artificial decontextualization and transfer of power, effects a break with biological time and place: housed in a form not its own, power can remain, for any period of time, impotent or ineffectual, inactive, or practically "dead." At the moments it is purposefully "unlocked" or "tapped" [*erschliessen*], released from containment in a delimited, directed fashion, its effectiveness can be redoubled, having been shaped by and brought to bear upon alien or extrinsic contexts. Thus our relationship to technology is obviously not that of individual subject to object, or even grammatical subject to predicate, discrete identities brought into temporary relationship by an action or verbal complement. Heidegger names that which is not a subject or something in itself, or is no longer, the "standing reserve" [*Bestand*], an assembled stock of means or elements kept accessible for eventual implementation. Like those "challenged" to bring it forth, and whom it challenges in turn, the standing reserve neither lives nor perishes on its own. It is the holding pattern whose concrete abstraction from the immediacy of living reveals "the real" of Being even as it destroys beings, the being of the Rhine as we know it or that of human beings subjected to the power their built technologies release and store.

"*What the river is now, namely, a water power supplier*": the renaming and redefining of something as a not-thing, a mechanism that stands in waiting, its interlocking, interactive parts available for implementation, is no mere polemical metaphor on Heidegger's part. In substituting an emphatically artificial compound word (*Wasserdrucklieferant*) for the natural fluidity of the being of the river, Heidegger brings to mind the larger mechanism this built network of operations, in effect, mimics, the mechanism that supplies the power to connect all objects and actions, with or without propinquity, to

---

stell" (roughly, "framing"), that which allows for, or puts into place, and so is neither precisely active nor receptive in origin (see "Frage," p. 35).

distinguish and distribute all attributes as well as command our attention to them. Lacking all natural foundation, *that mechanism is language*, the not-thing that "is" nothing other than the exercise of its forms and functions. Heidegger's concrete description of power artificially abstracted from given relations and conditions, transformed, housed, and directed not only with measurable efficacy but to inestimable, supplemental effect, is as illustrative a parable of the development of language as any characterizing those intellectual acts of modernization, which, before the isolation and distribution of electrical power, were collectively named the "enlightenment."[17] Recalling such materialist theorists of language and the machine as

17. Interestingly, Kant's famous 1784 essay on enlightenment, which analyzed and expanded the practical definition of the term to encompass the defining human "inclination and vocation to *think freely*" [*nämlich den Hang und Beruf zum* freien Denken], is entitled, like Heidegger's essay on technology, with a question ("Answer to the Question: What is Enlightenment?" [*Beantwortung der Frage: Was ist Aufklärung?*] (in Kant, *Werkausgabe*, XI:53–61, A 481–94 [61, A 494]). Although the question of enlightenment's definition was a topical one that had already been posed publicly—Moses Mendelssohn's response to it appearing in the *Berlinische Monatsschrift* in the same month Kant wrote his own (September 1784) (see Kant, *Werkausbage*, XI:61n, A 494n)—Kant's continued use of the term as an object of interrogation implies, as does Heidegger's "question of technology," that the very operation of the subject posed by the question is and will remain implicated in its answer: that understanding enlightenment requires what it itself entails, namely, a free, or nonfinite, process of thought. Kant's essay also ends by introducing the same distinction that Heidegger makes in "The Question Concerning Technology" (in his critique of Hegel and elsewhere) between human being and machine. While Heidegger emphasizes the nonautonomous status of the machine *viewed as technology*, that is, as a challenge brought forth by, and into enduring relation with, man, and Kant stresses the permanent challenge to human beings to "think freely" and to governments to "treat" people according to their "worth" *as* thinking beings, rather than as mere "machines" ("*den Menschen, der nun mehr als* Maschine *ist, seiner Würde gemäss zu behandeln*" [Kant, XI:61 A 494]), both Kant and Heidegger view the inherently active subjects of their analyses—the thinking underlying becoming enlightened and responding to technology, respectively—in opposition to any version of their mechanistic limitation and subordination, whether in the form of externally imposed tyranny

Condillac, Diderot, and La Mettrie, Heidegger's analysis of technology startles in its own enactment of "interlocking" concreteness and abstraction: the physical being of the river Rhine, given as such, is also given over to the "essence" of the water power plant into which it is "built" [*verbaut*], and of which it thus appears not the occasion but the effect. Indeed, the essence of that "essence" seems to be metalepsis, the poetic reversal of cause and effect, by which what the Rhine "is"—a natural source and place of power—"now" "derives" instead from its functional translation, just as the power of technology owes less to the river than to its own irreversible poetic process, that of exchanging organic nature for its organization and, in so doing, changing self-governing matter into material text and context.

The notion of essential translation pertains as much to the mechanization of *physis*, the natural repositories of energy in the world, as to the conduits and collecting stations, or grammar and words, which compose the mechanics of discourse and whose essence translates *psyche*, that uniquely human energy, into the world, forming and so transforming it, encoding and storing it, for present and future appropriation. It is not difficult, but rather difficult *not* to read in Heidegger's "standing reserve" the status and structure of language itself, of language that "is" what language does, the modality that not only changes the force of meaning it transfers, giving it shape, value, sense, and name, but also alters both ends of its own trajectory, the given context it leaves as well as that it makes. This is language not as "river," a unidirectional flow, spontaneous expression or act, but language as "water-power-supplier," as articulation and *metapherein*: the activity of identifying, containing, and relocating the power of meaning in a script, by means of which that power reemerges at once decontextualized and recontextualized, with or without either a proximate or referential basis. Unforeseeable in its destination and effects, such a distribution of power, while independent of nature, may carry with it at any time some or all of an

---

or self-deluding, means-to-an-end rationalization. (On enlightenment as ongoing, temporal action, see Kant, XI:59, A 491: "Do we now live in an *enlightened* age? . . . No, but we do live in an age of *enlightenment*."

acquired semantic sediment. Thus it is that the ungrounded technology of language, of storing and releasing energy by way of mechanisms that are always standing by, "on hand," defines, as it defies, the ratiocination of its "users" rather than the reverse.

While Heidegger is no more apologetic than Philomen and Baucis for his own enduring attachment to the earth, his questioning of technology removes the latter irrevocably from the realm of practiced, physical interaction with nature eulogized in this essay and others, that which, adhering to the ritual use of "hand tools" [*Werkzeuge*], links the body of nature and the human body across and through their difference, mutual resistance and submission.[18] Yet, it is in technology that Heidegger also recognizes the "*physis*" of that formative power that is and has always been at work in the world, the power to transform and reveal "also" named, he states, "*poiesis*," indicating, thereby, not only the congruence of technology and language, but the incongruous or exceptional identity of "poetry-making" torn between *techne* and *physis*, "water-power supplier" [*Wasserdrucklieferant*] and "hand tool" [*Werkzeug*].[19]

It is in this context that the essay most closely related to, and sharply differing from, "*Die Frage nach der Technik*," Heidegger's "*Ursprung des Kunstwerks*" (written 1935–36) must be read. Evoked

18. Similar to Benjamin's differentiation between "practiced," haptic or "tactile" experience and the temporal and spatial dislocation of experience produced with optical technologies (see, in particular, Benjamin, "Das Kunstwerk im Zeitalter seiner technischen Reproduzierbarkeit" and "Über einige Motive bei Baudelaire," in *Illuminationen*, pp. 136–69, 185–229 [esp. pp. 166–67, 221]; *Illuminations*, pp. 155–200, 217–51 [esp. pp. 186, 240]), Heidegger's long unraveling of the categories related in Hegelian dialectic, as of the mode of dialectical opposition itself, is effectively telegraphed in his passing, parenthetical differentiation between the manual *Werkzeug* and technology in this essay: "(Here would be the place to discuss Hegel's definition of the machine as an autonomous tool. With regard to the tool of manual work his characterization is right. Yet this does not think the machine on the basis of technology to which it belongs. Seen in terms of the standing reserve, the machine is completely nonautonomous; for it has its standing only from the ordering of the orderable)" (Heidegger, "Die Frage nach der Technik," pp. 16–17.

19. "*Physis*, the arising of something from out of itself, is also a bring-forth, *poiesis*"; "once the bringing-forth of the true into the beautiful was called

in a series of descriptions of precisely such practiced handwork as technology is here said to replace, works of art constitute *poiesis* in that earlier essay not as original, dislocating *techne* but rather as the lived-in, historical locus of Being, "wohnen" ("residing"). Between them the two essays effectively split Heidegger's conception of *poiesis* into a poetry of earth and a poetry of language, an architecture for dwelling and the uninhabitable architectonics of the moving and storing machine. This is not to say that Heidegger's conception of *poiesis* is either too capacious or self-negating, but rather that the work of art resembles *poiesis* as residing while technology resembles *poiesis* as power plant, as radically *non*residential building.[20] Thus, part of what Heidegger's unearthing of *poiesis* as mode of revealing or bringing forth reveals is that *poiesis* itself is not itself but rather Janus-like in its manifestations, place of Being or no-place, lined hand tool bearing traces of the work of historical bodies on earth or temporary storage facility for a power extracted from the earth and necessarily isolated from bodies it can kill, a power put on indefinite hold rather than ever held and implemented by hand.

IT IS EXACTLY these two faces of Heidegger's *poiesis*—being of, and not of, the earth and laboring hand—that are conjoined to awful effect in the carrying out of Faust's materialist architectonic plan. For the "hands," Faust commands work not like hands but like power-suppliers, mechanisms for a transfer of energy occurring at the cost of the bodies from which it derives. Here the "hands" working to remove and replace the earth to which they are enslaved are themselves *Werkzeuge*, but these are "hand tools" implemented in the mode of nonmanual technology, with all the violence—to body and to earth—that conflating these two mutually unidentifiable ways of *poiesis* entails.

---

techne. *Techne* was also called the *poiesis* of the beautiful arts" (Heidegger, "Die Frage nach der Technik," pp. 15, 38).

20. The split between *techne* and *poiesis* is discussed as historically formative of Heidegger's own course of thought by Gabriel Riera, in *Intrigues*, pp. 48–52. See the continuation of this note in the Appendix.

Extraction, transformation, storage, distribution, exchange or switching—modes of managing the energy concealed in and composing the relations of nature—belong, for Heidegger, to the realm of "bringing forth" that may indeed be named for the essence or metalepsis of language, *metapherein* (generally, "to move, to transfer"); for language, not as nominal substitution for a nonlinguistic realm, but rather, as mode of appropriating, articulating, and revealing that realm by directing, as it defines, the power of understanding. Unruly at first, imposing and winning by design, metaphor is language, the "natural" flow of grammar and syntax, as technology is *bios*, the naturally flowing Rhine, under new management.

Just as Faust's rejection of the "old" forms of language for the immediacy of sensuous life turns inevitably into a rejection of the "old" earth upon which sensuous experience transpires, so Faust's architectonic reconstitution of the earth, *not with but as technology*[21]—as power-supplier that, like language, breaks "new" ground

21. Cf. Jeffrey Barnouw, "Faust and the Ethos of Technology," pp. 29–42, in which Faust's building project is accurately interpreted as viewed by Faust himself as "a technological marvel" and, somewhat less accurately, as "a large-scale housing project" (37), the latter based on the single line, "the peoples' expansive residence" [*Der Völker breiten Wohngewinn*] (*Faust II*, V.11250), within Faust's long lament of the obstruction caused by the lindens to his exhaustive vision of what he [*ich*]—conceived to subsume the work of "a thousand hands"—has built: "The few trees that are not mine / Spoil for me my possession of the world. / There, in order to look far around, I wanted / To build scaffolding from tree to tree, / To open a wide path for the eye / To see, all that I have done, / To look over with a single glance / The masterpiece of the human spirit / To activate with intelligence / The peoples' expansive residence." [*Die wenig Bäume, nicht mein eigen, / Verderben mir den Weltbesitz. / Dort wollt'ich, weit umherzuschauen, / Von Ast zu Ast Gerüste bauen, / Dem Blick eröffnen weite Bahn, / Zu sehn, was alles ich getan, / Zu überschauen mit einem Blick / Des Menschengeistes Meisterstück, / Betätigend mit klugem Sinn / Der Völker breiten Wohngewinn*] (*Faust II*, V.11241–50). While Barnouw's conclusion, that, "in his expansive 'striving,' Faust embodies an indifference to our vulnerability and fallibility," is, again, both accurate, and the very least one can say, the present argument suggests that Faust's brutal building project aims to establish, by disentangling it from the earth, less a particular structure than the "free ground," which is that of technology itself.

by breaking the natural chain of cause and effect—must destroy the life that constitutes the earth in order to channel it. Replacing the earth with a "new earth," the old encumbered ground with a "free ground," Faust builds not earth but the freedom from earth that is technology. Technology, a non-being, "is" the new basis for freedom, and sole basis for defining the "new" because its functioning constitutes its own ground precisely by freeing itself from earthly constraints. Rather than a body or an idea, technology dazzlingly embodies the break with bodies and ideas, the caesura that allows these to be stored and transferred at will. Indifferent to any difference between discursivity and sensuousness—and, within these, to historicity and individuality, their strangeness *and* familiarity—technology is defined by a rapidity outstripping the labor of both hand and eye, of tactile contact and cognitive communication alike. In this it will indeed always be "new," and in this, too, it proves ultimately unmanageable for Faust, an undoing of time exceeding even Faust's restless vision.

3. In the Place of Language

FOR, EVEN IN succeeding, such "new" management cannot break even. Once unmoored and moved about, power inevitably gets "out of hand" in the figurative as well as literal sense, transgressing the limit of its separation from earth, the same separation enabling its orientation toward an end. If "language" is another word for "technology" in Heidegger's analysis, or what Heidegger here and elsewhere calls *poiesis*, then another word for the transgression of the limit separating earth and technology is "time." Time alone can reveal the enduring difference between river and water-power-supplier, time which is itself brought to the fore by the activity of *metapherein* on earth, the forceful rewriting of physical cause and effect. And these are precisely the terms of being on earth that Faust's building project, at first, reverses.

For, *in building a ground*, Faust would instead *sunder earth and time in the mode of technology*. His aim is not to monumentalize, to contain and mark the place of the body of a god on earth whose title in life, "Pharoh," already signified the "Great House" of a deathless being. Nor does he build to contain in the form of a symbol or statue a literary and historical turning point, a riddle for an Oedipus at a crossroads, the solution of which tells human time as a three-part story and allows Oedipus's own narrative *mythos* and dramatic *peripeteia* to proceed. Pyramid and sphinx, the original embodiments of the semiotic outer limits of Hegel's tale of the aesthetic—of the arbitrary sign becoming symbol and symbol reverting to arbitrary sign over time, sensuous versions of the narrative of "unification-" "turning-" and "departure-point(s)" the *Aesthetics* ascribes to "freedom" in "Kantian philosophy"—these built forms stand for "nothing" (in the sense Kant describes[22]) more than time; and, no less important, at dawn, at noon, *and* at dusk, unlike humans (so the riddle of the Sphinx), *they stand*. Rising and extending from earth into air, they are the negative image of the invisible "framework" that allows but does not house all technologies, the uncontainable basis of being on earth, temporality.

In building a form of technology instead of a building, the only form of building that could make theory at once praxis, Faust constructs an earth that usurps the earth, an origin uninvolved in temporality. And yet, as Heidegger's analysis of technology suggests, it is the act of building as replacement and reversal of earth-bound cause and effect, that, in subtracting temporality, as it extracts power, from the earth, will cause earthly time to reassert itself with unnatural force.[23] So it is for Faust: beholding the "newest earth" [*neust(e) Erde*] and "space of millions" [*Räume vielen Millionen*] his reshaping of the earth's surface first "opens" [*(e)röffn'*] to view (*Faust II*, V.11563–66), Faust takes a step forward *in time*, which is at once a step toward archaeology. Looking ahead he unearths the words whose reiteration condemns him (by his own words) to death, the expression of the desire that time not transpire addressed to the condition of passing time itself: "Should I to the moment say: / abide a while! You are so beautiful! / Then you may slap chains on me, / Then will I gladly go

22. Kant, *KrV*, B 51, III:81: "When we abstract from our mode of intuiting ourselves internally, and also of considering, by way of this intuition, all external intuitions in the power of representation, and consequently take from this mode all objects, such as they may be in themselves, so is time nothing."

23. By contrast—as Riera accurately points out—when writing on the origin of the work of art, Heidegger produces a "discourse . . . on what exceeds the place and truth itself, a discourse on *spacing*" (Riera, *Intrigues*, p. 73). It is at the inevitable, perceptual moment that Faust's *techne* of building as technology rejoins and redefines the earth *as a place*—a moment of seeing something "new" that, recalling an old desire for such vision, is commemorated in language that can only be citational—that "*spacing*" as such, a pure, entirely noncommemorative, technologically engendered production of self-differing spatiality, intersects instead with temporality, and Goethe's literary drama departs from the exclusively ontological treatment of the work of art that marks Heidegger's early attempt to equate, while subordinating, *techne* to *poiesis*.

to my destruction!" [*Werd' ich zum Augenblicke sagen: / Verweile doch! Du bist so schön! / Dann magst du mich in Fesseln schlagen, / Dann will ich gern zugrunde gehn!*] (*Faust I*, 1699–1702).

Ironically, it is not the new empirical reality presented to the eye by the construction of canals for transportation and of solid ground from shifting water—the refashioning of earth into technology, the basis for freedom from all sensuous temporality—but the entirely imaginary reality of future "freedom" to be "conquered daily" upon this built foundation (*Faust II*, V.11576) that appears to make Faust forget he is not speaking entirely in the present; that, in stating what he would say in the face of such a hypothetical future state, he is restating what he *had* said would spell the loss of his wager.[24] Envisioning an unfathomable freedom of action grounded ultimately upon this initial risk, Faust makes building an index of temporality, and in so doing reveals archaeology and architecture to be fraternal twins. The "origin" he has brought to "mind" (*arche-logos*) are the words long preceding the deeds that define where he is. And while

24. The open embrace of operatic artifice and of magic in *Faust I* and *II*, including the fabulous invention of "magic sheets of paper" [*Zauberblätter*] (*Faust II*, I.6157)—the all-powerful because purely symbolic currency of intrinsically worthless, printed money—that have been commented on insightfully by others (see esp. Brown, *Goethe's Faust*, pp. 135–52, 208–13, 225–29, *et passim*; Kaiser, *Ist der Mensch zu Retten?* pp.25–38 ["Paper money turns into the secular symbol of salvation" (29)]; Binswanger, *Geld und Magie*, esp. pp. 167–71; Schell, "Money and the Mind" p. 58), may be seen as positive, allegorical representations of the fatality of language *and* of history when the two are either arbitrarily *or* instrumentally severed. Faust's return to language, articulated and represented in the specifically verbal form of the sentence he has wagered he will have no desire to say, is also a return to the making of history, not in the form of the dead and deadly letter language inevitably becomes (no saving "eternal feminine" waiting in the wings to draw it erotically into immortality), but in the formation of a referent, a "free ground" that founds no utopia, aesthetic or otherwise, but, on the contrary, the very possibility of the presently invisible, of history eradicated and history to come. On the "ambivalence" toward language enacted by Goethe in *Faust*, see Sussman, "The Economics of Translation in *Faust*," pp. 177, 179, 181; on the "meaninglessness" of "history, as it is conceived in *Faust* . . . of itself," see Brown, *Goethe's Faust*, 195.

actions "take place in," define, or ground the present, words are always only present in part, as repetitions of themselves, as representations of what they are not. By the same token, any foreknowledge of the basis upon which actions occur can make acts taking place in the present resemble language too much, repetitions of other actions, representations of extraneous aims.

Thus, in order to effect what his early revision of the Old Testament merely proposed—to "begin" ("*Im Anfang* . . .") with the "act" ("... *war die Tat*") rather than the "word" (*Faust I*, 1224–37)—Faust had finally to construct a ground that had never been seen or acted upon before. To that end, he signed himself over to what appeared an inestimably profitable exchange: the bartering of a phrase, in the form of its quotation, for constantly changing experience; the trading of recognizable and thus deathly verbal delimitation ("The word already dies in the pen" [*Das Wort erstirbt schon in der Feder*] [*Faust I*, 1728]), for the life of unknown, unlimited action ("Let us crash into the rush of time, into the rolling of the given! . . . Man can only be active without rest" [*Stürtzen wir uns in das Rauschen der Zeit, / Ins Rollen der Begebenheit! . . . Nur rastlos betätigt sich der Mann*] [*Faust I*, 1754–59]). An exchange, however, remains an exchange, which is to say, linguistic at its core, and the winner's bargain Faust strikes must be and is undone by its original *and* repetitive form. An earth newly wrenched from non-earth would yield the unbiased basis, he speculates, for a "free people," and it is his active "anticipation" [*Vorgefühl*], rather than actual vision, both of a world unmarked by past history and of his own historical inscription in its surface henceforth—the indelible "trace" of his own "days on earth" that he trusts building to leave in history to come—that usurps the ceaseless pursuit of present action to which Faust had sworn himself in Part I:

> Such a crowd I'd like to see,
> To stand on a free foundation with a free people.
> To the moment I should say:
> Linger a while, you are so beautiful!
> The trace of my days on earth
> Cannot be destroyed in the aeons.

In anticipation of such high happiness
I now enjoy the highest moment.
(*Faust sinks back, the lemurs grab him and lay him on the ground.*)

[Solch ein Gewimmel möcht' ich sehn,
Auf freiem Grund mit freiem Volke stehn.
Zum Augenblicke dürft' ich sagen:
Verweile doch, du bist so schön!
Es kann die Spur von meinen Erdetagen
Nicht in Äonen untergehn.—
Im Vorgefühl von solchem hohen Glück
Geniess' ich jetzt den höchsten Augenblick.
(*Faust sinkt zurück, die Lemuren fassen ihn auf und legen ihn auf den Boden.*)]

(*Faust II*, V.11579–86)

Faust speaks his own loss of the present, loses himself to words he had used in the past to indicate future closure, and he does so on the very ground, the "free foundation," he has constructed to ensure a permanent present. And so, too, in a sense, he makes the moment linger—not by extending the present (into the future or nonpresent) but by verbally collapsing future, present, and past. Just as building materially opposes the "whirl of time" [*das Rauschen der Zeit*] (*Faust I*, 1754) with which Faust had wished to merge, in a seamless interplay of natural sensuousness and artifice endowing his individual experiences with the absolute freedom of timelessness—the timelessness of constant change, of time itself—so building, in marking a place in the earth that had been only earth and no place before, in establishing the location of a technology separating power from the earth, makes Faust yearn differently: not for his own merger into "the rolling round of the given" [*ins Rollen der Begebenheit*] (*Faust I*, 1755), but for the joining of that which was never naturally or artificially given before—the "new earth" or *techne* he has *made* from matter—with sensuously bound experience, the individual experience of seeing a "free people" whose momentary beauty as such he would wish to have linger.[25] Faust, the creature freed, by his own words renouncing words, from the cognitive and experiential constraints of time and space, has built a "new earth," a "ground" for storing and transporting energy that is indeed "free," free that is, to become a place and basis for future experience and cognition, free to serve the future as its referent.

25. Without commenting on the architectural basis of Faust's desired union of "freedom" with experience, Lange recognizes that Faust's "project[ed]" "vision" of a "utopia" foresees a place disengaged specifically from "history," even as he comes short of acknowledging that it is the actual viewing of this "utopia," the "glimpse" of his own vision concretely realized as a material place, that at once destroys its quality as a no-place and returns Faust to temporality: "in a vision of an idyllic-paradisal life . . . Faust projects the utopia of a life that is free from the paralyzing consciousness of one's own insufficiencies . . . free also of the debasement of man by nature and history. The achievement of 'standing with a free people on a free foundation' (V. 11580) would be the goal of a great creative project, through which the experience of temporality could be overcome, its magically compelling character transcended" (Lange, "*Faust*," p. 306).

4. "Time Refound"

THE RECOVERY OF TIME in the loss of life may seem, from the point of view of individual experience, an oxymoron. From the point of view of literary representation—or rather, from within the long view literature labors to represent—to re-find time is to measure the life, and thus the death, of experience, and in no literary work is that equation carried out more consistently, at greater length, or in more precise detail than in Proust's *À la recherche du temps perdu*, the monumental work that, considered from a certain, abbreviated perspective it offers to view, can help illuminate and introduce Goethe's remarkably un-Faust-like novel, a story of life that rather, mysteriously, requires building, *Die Wahlverwandtschaften*.

While the stated ambitions of Proust's narrator, "Marcel," and Goethe's dramatic character could hardly be more different—the one seeking to remember and possess in permanent form what the other wants only to forget—both Proust's novel and Goethe's drama represent the conflict between experience and time in the form of something that belongs to neither and serves both alternately. Marking time while negating experience and vice versa, it is only in this fundamentally equivocal sense that building can be said to mediate between them. It is through this double-edged mediation of the architectural, however, that the relation between *Faust*, in which building provides the basis for the final words of the "hero" of a markedly artificial drama, and *Die Wahlverwandtschaften*, in which building provides the basis for the first words of a "realist" fiction, may perhaps be glimpsed.

For, recalling and contradicting Faust is the original *dramatis persona* of Proust's novel of "time lost" and "refound," the character whom Marcel claims as both his model in life and countermodel in art, Swann. It is the famous, self-declared fate of Swann, unlike that of the narrator who states at the end of this circular work his intention to become a writer, to have "wasted years of [his] life, to have wanted to die, to have had [his] greatest love, for a woman [he] didn't like, who was not of [his] *genre*."[26] Yet it is also Swann who first constructs the ground, in constructing the "*architecture*," of that wasted life when he builds in memory a foundation for its future from the groundless movement, waves or "*flots*" of music he had loved and lost, and which he heard again in this woman's presence.[27] Swann's notational construction of memory secures its performance while obliterating its object, actual sensory experience itself, making the fleeting sonoric tides of the Vinteuil Sonata as visibly present as a "thing . . . of architecture," while rendering the mysterious sensuousness of the music a thing of the past.[28]

The purpose of Faust's, unlike Swann's "architecture" is, however, precisely *not* to remember, not to relive or capture but rather to discard without trace sensory experience now past. Faust builds a foundation on moving waters so as to make memory itself a thing of the past and the present a thing of the future. In so doing he ends up repeating the words that make "Faust" as *dramatis persona* a thing of the past instead. Recalling words of his own composition, and whose utterance his whole freedom put off, Faust as builder finds himself wedded to his own wager, saying I do (want the instant to linger) to his own proposal (that he will not).

Having passionately sought a composition he could not recall, and in whose identification and permanent notation his freedom is lost, Proust's Swann too ends up wedded to a citation, but without divine intervention to "pull him on." Instead, this most anti-Faustian character in fiction knowingly marries a *form* of the eternal feminine

26. Proust, *À la recherche*, I:382.

27. Ibid., I:209 (emphasis added). I have discussed Proust's description of memory, which, "like a laborer working to establish durable foundations in the middle of tides," constructs an "architecture" unrelated to either voluntary or involuntary memory, in "Remembering Swann"; see also Chap. 7, and Coda of *The Imposition of Form*.

28. Proust, *À la recherche*, I:382.

itself. Being pulled down by lemurs may be no worse than being married to the very body of quotation, Odette; of that life we can surmise little, and Swann himself, as reported by the narrator who creates him, would have had least to say. Consigned to repeat a "phrase" that is no longer living, Swann's is a life indeed lived, as his narrator remarks, "between quotation marks," life's own negation—a daily inscription upon ongoing sensory experience of the mental transcription of immediate sensory experience by architecturally made memory—and the content of such experience, like the content of Odette, must remain, strictly speaking, incomparable with any other hell.[29]

The made thing that presages the negation of life and advent of literature, that renders posthumous or citational the enlivening, purely present experience it was intended to secure, is architectural in form. For Faust and anti-Faust alike, the difference between the desire to experience sensuous life positively, over and over, in the present, and the fatal state of possession that ensures life is never present, always lost, is neither a matter of "words," nor of "deeds," nor even of their supposed opposition. It is a built thing that, different from each of these, joins them both negatively and positively—which is to say, in the long view, both historically and poetically—to each other in time. And it is the omnipresence of building, rather than its construction to ensure a specific, sensory present, that Goethe's *Wahlverwandtschaften* makes the foundation of historical experience, its knowledge and its loss.

29. Ibid., I:98.

PART II

Built Time

But should we not build something more upon it?
[*Sollen wir aber nichts weiter darauf bauen?*]

EDUARD, in *Die Wahlverwandtschaften*

The intervening time had fallen into oblivion.
[*Die Zwischenzeit war ins Vergessen gefallen.*]

Die Wahlverwandtschaften

1. Building, Story, and Image

THE EXPERIENCE OF *Wahlverwandtschaften* is the eradication of time—of "something" that is, in itself, nothing—and the activity that brings about the occasion for this obliteration is, ironically, the making of something in the place of "nothing," building.[1] As described by the characters that embody it, the notion of *Wahlverwandtschaften*—"chosen" [*wahl*] but involuntary, improper but fitting "relations" [*verwandtschaften*]—constitutes a "misleading" "metaphor" for human and nonhuman interactions alike.[2] As a general term for the forging of a new relation from discrete entities, *Wahlverwandtschaften* appears a false representation of any particular relation it names; such is the fate of any metaphor for metaphor, the give-and-take of figural relations, a fate shared by the crisscrossed lovers of the novel themselves.[3] Yet building, the endeavor which brings those characters together in the first place, not only literally setting the scene but establishing the very theater

1. "Nothing" here is not another name for nature, but indicates rather no thing, i.e., no object, product or entity, of human making or conception. Building may order or re-order, stand for, or add to such things, but, in order to materialize as such, building must *take place* in the most literal—which is to say, concrete—sense, demarcating and constructing form in a space where no thing already is.

2. Johann Wolfgang von Goethe, *Die Wahlverwandtschaften: Ein Roman*, in Goethe, *Werke*, VI:270–75. All subsequent quotations are from this edition. See the continuation of this note in the Appendix.

3. On "Wahlverwandtschaften" as "Metapher für die Metaphor" (a metaphor for metaphor), see Thomas Fries, *Die Wirklichkeit der Literatur*, p. 100. See the continuation of this note in the Appendix.

for their appearance, is not—even metaphorically speaking—a metaphor.[4] In itself, building neither compares, nor substitutes, nor exchanges: it is not a structure for making meaning out of the logical conceptual tradeoffs (implicit for explicit, part for whole, absent for present, among the most frequent) engendered by every metaphor's double, or conventional and unconventional, reference. Building is instead the making of a structure out of materials having physical-mathematical, but no referential, function. Precisely because its component parts are independent of reference, building is as concrete as metaphor is fictive or immaterial, which is to say that the referentiality of metaphor, like its duplicity, is operative in language alone. In short, while a metaphor is solely conceived as such because of its apparent meanings, whatever a building may appear to "mean" has no bearing upon its being building.

Peculiar to *Die Wahlverwandtschaften*, however, is its emphatic foregrounding of *both* metaphoric and architectural activity, whose co-presence, bordering on interdependence, brings the fundamental question of this study—that of the relationship of building to language—center stage. In steering clear of any synthesis or analogy between them, while making these modes of construction, more than its explicitly cipher-like characters, the main performers of its plot, the novel presents, in seamless literary form, not so much a story of bourgeois *Sitten* in conflict with irrational passions, as a masterful remix of Hegel's history of spirit brought to consciousness and

4. The nonmetaphoric status of building in the novel is related to but not identifiable with Heidegger's remarkable assertion, in the *Letter on Humanism*, that to name that which "thinking builds upon" "the house of Being" is "no figural transfer of the image of the 'house' onto Being"; see Martin Heidegger, *Platons Lehre von Wahrheit*, p. 111; see also pp. 115–16: "'Stay' means in our language 'keeping' (or 'custody'). Being is the keeping that watches over man in his ex-istent essence in the way of its truth such that it houses ex-istence in language. That is why language it at once the house of Being and the housing of human essence. Ex-istence resides, thinking, in the house of Being." See also *Identität und Differenz*, p. 104: "In the event of appropriation oscillates the essence of that which speaks as language, language which once was called the house of Being."

advanced by way of different art forms.[5] The plot of *Die Wahlverwandtschaften* requires both building and "chosen relations" to develop, and these require each other if each is to occur at all, yet the two activities (and here one has no choice but to speak figuratively) do not "speak the same language": while figural relations, as the novel demonstrates, are always partly extrinsically motivated and thus intrinsically unstable, pointing toward something absent or foreign to the context at hand, architectural relations can only exist in equilibrium and are by definition self-containing.

Still, from beginning to end, the story of illicit or improperly directed passions *Die Wahlverwandtschaften* metaphorically names, rises and falls with the structures of increasing signification erected on Eduard's grounds.[6] The more or less overt sexual "dimension" of such building is but one of its representational connotations, not its cause. Once "Eduard," the opening word of the novel, is arbitrarily

5. While Goethe elsewhere defined "the architectonic" as that "productive," "constitutive" "power" whose absence defines dilettantism (See "Über den Dilettantismus," manuscript dated 3 March 1799, in Goethe, *Gedenkausgabe* [754]), and famously declared *Die Wahlverwandtschaften* "the only product of extensive dimension in which I worked consciously to represent a single thoroughgoing idea" (Goethe to Eckermann, 6 May 1827, Härtl, ed. *Eine Dokumentation*, p. 327), the conspicuousness with which the novel and its represented relations are grounded a priori, and ad infinitum, in all species of architectonic activity has been considered only once, to my knowledge, in modern critical literature (see Dickson, discussed shortly). Perhaps because its self-evidence bears with it no evident meaning, the foregrounding of the architectonic impulse in the novel was judged a puzzling, even annoying distraction by some of its most celebrated early readers. See the continuation of this note in the Appendix.

6. See Keith A. Dickson's recognition, in "Spatial Concentration and Themes," that, with few exceptions, "the entire action of Goethe's novel is restricted to the dominant topographical features of a nobleman's estate . . . everything which happens elsewhere is 'off the map' and therefore totally irrelevant to the action of [the] novel . . . Off the estate the characters are out of focus" (159–61). Dickson further suggests the abstract rather than realistic significance of the novel's "domination" by architectural activity in remarking on the "complete anonymity" of the region in which it takes place (161).

set down, its content defined by a self-nominating narrative voice ("Eduard—so we name a rich Baron in the best years of his life . . .") and then, having been "so" predicated, restated as a subject and basis for narration ("—Eduard had . . ."), the narrative identifies its first, explicitly linguistically constructed subject with the explicitly artificial construction in which he is situated (". . . spent the prettiest hour of an April afternoon in his botanical nursery . . .") If the random designation, "Eduard," is defined from the outset to signify the representation of a generic type, the landed gentry, the immediate condition of its further fictional particularization is neither a natural nor a social context, but a building built for engineering nature.

As if imitating, against all probability, the complex experience of an actual building, the act of building produces from the start of the novel both its surface and its depth, its descriptive setting or *mimesis* as well as its momentum, *mythos*, or plot.[7] Just as a building creates a depth or interior no less artificial and arbitrary, or unnaturally motivated, than its outside shell, and just as the furnishings of those "interiors" are finally only another layer of externals within externals, an object-laden content functioning uncannily as yet another context, so we recognize that the very activity of constructing something in the novel has the function not only of moving its story forward but of making the setting and internal motivation of its characters' actions appear, if not identical, at least two sides of the same wall.[8]

7. Cf. Christian Scharf's related observation, in *Goethes Ästhetik*, that the "landscape" that constitutes the "surface" of the novel "slowly loses its own value as fictional element" and becomes instead "a symbol of the course of the narrative" (220).

8. For a related discussion of the non-internal quality of built "interiors"—human and otherwise—in realist literature, see my "Narrate or Educate: *Le Père Goriot* and the Realist Bildungsroman." The comparison of the two novels sheds light on both in revealing an important distinction between Balzacian realist prose and Goethe's prose rendering of figuration. While Goethe's novel lays and relays groundplans that appear co-extensive with human passion, representing the architectonic as the never perfected home of the figural, Balzac's near eradication of the distinction between "*intra*" and "*extra muros*," as between people and furniture, in the Maison Vauquer of *Le Père Goriot*, extends equally to all plot developments within and without the Maison, as to all ob-

Like his first narrated act, the solitary husbanding in a "Baumschule" of a new botanic composition, Eduard's first words serve simultaneously to introduce Charlotte and to position her within a place of her own making; asking his gardener whether he "has seen [his] wife," Eduard learns Charlotte is "in the new facilities" (VI:242) she has added to the grounds. The initial appearances of both Eduard and Charlotte as characters, then, take place within built contexts they have already engineered, contexts whose apparent differentiation (arboretum, buildings) serves only to render insignificant any categorical distinction between natural and architectural, organic and inorganic forms. While it is difficult to think of another novel in which the built more completely defines the view of the natural landscape, and the architectural, as *fait accompli* that is never quite finished, more conspicuously determines the narrative field, preceding physical and psychological description as well as development of narrative background, the unprecedented, ongoing engagement with building in the novel is and will remain unexplained within it.[9]

---

ject-laden contexts of action in Balzac. The passions of Balzac's characters level the difference between the inside and outside of people and places even as they take full inventory of the furnishings that inspire them; so Balzac, in narrating the ungoverned social mobility effected by those passions, levels the difference not between the social classes but between any supposedly inherent attributes that define them, and whose possession, loss, or acquisition he shows to inhere in nothing more intrinsic than the genius of mobility itself. See the continuation of this note in the Appendix.

9. Although he does not note their subordination to the architectural, H. G. Barnes compares the preponderant "descriptions" of "landscape" in the novel to their structural use as "functions of the action" in a novella, rather than as mere background detail (Barnes, *Goethe's Wahlverwandtschaften*, p. 9). Barnes emphasizes "the significance of place" in *Die Wahlverwandtschaften*, commenting instructively on "the mysterious relationship between landscape and character" that the narrator's "ironic," at once "concrete" and "reflective," "narrative style" effects (8–9). Yet his perception of the indivisible union in the novel of place and narration, as of the "concrete" and "reflect[ion]"—*grosso modo* the union of *Grundstein* with *Denkstein* discussed in sections four and five below—seems to lead Barnes to replace his own conception of the integral, compositional "function" of place in the novel with a supernatural view of both the novel and its landscape as "magical" in "function": "the repeated

Shorn of the logic of plot-related necessity or circumstance, and undetermined by social and historical factors that themselves remain unstated, the fact of the characters' architectural exercises is fully narrated, but never narratively motivated. At once abstract, or owing to no given external cause, and concrete, or participating in the external world, these ungrounded architectonic acts act as the novel's own foundation, the basis of its characters' presentation and their first verbal exchange, including Eduard's pivotal, if recursive, suggestion that building, once begun, requires more building: "but should we not build something more upon it?" It is this baseless supposition regarding building, asserted as if self-evident, in the guise or rhetoric of a question, that, as discussed later in this section, inaugurates the relay of wayward events that give rise to the novel's "relations," providing, at once literally and figuratively, the grounds on which they are based.

That relay or relation of events makes itself known without delay. While "Eduard'"s nearly Euclidian introduction ("let *a* designate a quantity such that . . .") identifies him from the outset as no one in particular, a proper noun plucked from nowhere to occupy a position of centrality to a plot, Charlotte's location off-stage identifies her immediately with a building site to which Eduard then repairs, the "Mooshütte" (moss hut) she is said to have "finished" "buil[ding]" that day, and at whose "door" she is first named: "At the door Charlotte received her husband . . ." (VI:242–43). Any reader familiar enough with the larger thicket of the novel to linger over this early,

---

reference to objects in the landscape, without, however, vouchsafing further detail as to their appearance, tends to endow them with a mysterious, highly suggestive character. In consequence, their enumeration soon assumes the function of a magic formula and the reader before long envisages the characters as moving in a charmed world" (74). This "charmed," "mysterious[ly] . . . suggestive" "world" is later summarized by Barnes as a "landscape of passion" (82). Without noting the extent to which "landscape" in the novel is understood a priori by its narrator and characters as the medium and product of construction, Barnes had already remarked in an earlier essay on its active role in the novel's "ambiguous" events; see Barnes, "Bildhafte Darstellung": "Landscape also enters the actions and participates in its ambiguous course" (45).

architectonic detail will recognize it as the model for that later, intimate "reception" of Eduard, which serves to illustrate, indeed almost picture, the ambiguous referentiality and consequent impropriety of the novel's title, when one evening it is, in Charlotte's mind, not Eduard but the absent Hauptmann who stands before her door ("The figure of the Hauptmann stood before the door"), not Eduard but the absent Hauptmann whom she receives in accordance with "inner inclination" (VI:321). Innocent, for the moment, of such figural complication, this first scene of meeting between husband and wife is, however, also architecturally mediated, defined and framed by the built opening that stands between them.[10]

The spousal, quasi-natural "moss hut" is soon related to further-reaching architectural designs whose conception and realization compose the scenes and content of the entire course of the novel's progress. Its "groundstone-laying" and completed "construction" made to commemorate Charlotte's and Ottilie's birthdays by the Hauptmann and Eduard respectively, the larger *Lustgebäude* (lodge, pavilion, or recreational house; literally, "pleasure-building") planned and executed by the Hauptmann rapidly supplants Charlotte's rustic retreat *à deux* (VI:296, 335). The "violence" of Ottilie's

10. The intertwining of architecture, image, and story in the novel already informs the first narrated encounter of husband and wife, in that the "different images" Charlotte next bids Eduard view from within the moss hut are, in fact, glimpses of nature composed—formed and framed—by the "door and windows" she has had built, just as it is the putative "narrowness" of the hut itself that provides the pretext for Eduard's and Charlotte's first narrated conversation, in which Eduard expresses and defends his desire to have a "friend" help him survey and map the estate. The act of surveying swiftly yields to the activity of "build[ing] further" in Eduard's subsequent exchange with Charlotte, who, in turn, agrees to invite the Hauptmann, and, thus, implicitly, to continue building, on the condition that she may invite Ottilie, and so on, until the story's nominal and, as always, architecturally contextualized end, when, Eduard and "the heavenly" Ottilie now permanently installed beneath a painted heavenly vault, the narrative predicts "the happy moment" when they will "awaken together again" (VI:243–47, 490).

While overlooking their shared involvement with the architectural, several valuable studies have commented on the relationship of images to story in the novel. See the continuation of this note in the Appendix.

future attempt to reach that new building in haste, her doomed imitation, by bodily motion, of the instantaneous traversal of space by "the eyes" and "mind," will later bring about Otto's death-day and the beginning of the post-mortem period of the relations that bore him (VI:456–57). "The house and household affairs" to which Ottilie devotes herself "more than to the world, more than to the life outdoors" provide the self-containing interior in whose confines she begins to mirror Eduard physically and within which, upon departing, he insists she remain, so that, absent his living person, the presence of his structure for living—his building—may continue to define her (VI:296, 344). The "little-noticed side-chapel" the architect plans to make "a memorial of earlier times" by copying onto its vaulted ceiling "antique" "figures" from his itinerant funerary collection, becomes adorned instead by renderings of Ottilie's face set in an "azure heaven," with the effect that, at the close of the novel, not only the transcription of figural representations of death but the very idea of death is abandoned, as it is instead "Ottilie herself" who "appears to look down from the heavenly spaces" upon her own "glass-covered" body below (VI:366–67, 372, 485).[11]

Finally, a large bequest to the church from Charlotte ensures Ottilie and Eduard will lie "side by side" beneath that curved canopy in perpetuity, the painted "gaze" of "imaged angels" and "peace hang[ing] over their abode" (VI:490).[12] Thus the long-neglected side-building, brought back to life by the architect, ultimately houses the

11. On the novel's obfuscation of death though visual imaging, cf. Hermann, *Die Todesproblematik*, and Jutta Steinbiss's observation, in *Der "freundliche Augenblick,"* that the pictoral imaging of Ottilie allows her to appear "simultaneous to three time periods," the time previous to the novel, the time of the novel's events, and the stoppage of time in "eternity" (103).

12. This voluntary perpetuation by Charlotte of the visibility and contiguity of the dead bodies of *Wahlverwandtschaften* defies not only the abstract bent of the erasure of burial places in the church graveyard she is said to have initiated *before* the onset of those relations (see section four), but any notion that architectural activity in the novel functions merely as psychological reflection of and compensation for the inadequacies of Charlotte's "marital relation" with Eduard, the conclusion Dickson reaches in his otherwise penetrating essay when he states: "developing the estate is a kind of therapeutic substitute for

deceased lovers in a kind of immortality. The narration of their relation ends with its only possible final representation, that of an afterworld rendered redundant by its own earthly architectonic embodiment, a rounded enclosure proffering the portrait of infinite blessing in infinite space (VI:490). In order to complete their transfiguration from "*häuslich*" to "*heilig*," from household creatures to chapel saints, the protagonists of this novel merely require what they always required, "a friendly, quiet apartment" in which to reside (VI:296, 490, 485).[13] Their housing provides the basis for the continuation of a relation apparently undeterred by the difference between life and death.

The notion of housing Ottilie in the "apartment" the newly refurbished chapel is now said to provide is first advanced in order to persuade Eduard to permit her body to be separated from him and his surroundings. The suggestion achieves its desired end: Eduard allows Ottilie to be "laid to rest" [*biegesetzt*] in a specific, concrete sense. For, rather than interred beneath the ground, Ottilie will instead be set aside—the use of *beisetzen* here recalling *beiseitesetzen*—so as to "remain among the living" (VI:485). Yet Eduard's assent to installing Ottilie in the "side-chapel" "arch" is premised on the further "condition" that her body be made available to viewing

---

developing their own marital relation, which, like the estate, leaves much to be desired" (Dickson, "Spatial Concentration and Themes, p. 164.)

13. "Ottilie was instead already fully mistress of the household . . . Her entire way of thinking was oriented toward the house and household matters [*dem Häuslichen*], more than toward the world . . ." [VI:296]; " . . . and as (Eduard) fell asleep in thinking on the holy girl [*die Heilige*], so can he well be named blessed."

While importantly noting that it "was once a place in which the feasts of saints, i.e., the anniversaries of their deaths were celebrated," Barnes does not observe that the chapel in which Ottilie is installed for viewing has already been desacralized by what he calls "the art of the dilettante" of the architect, including, foremost, its decoration with images of Ottilie (Barnes, *Goethes Wahlverwandtschaften*, p. 80). Despite the display of her dead body in a residence described as of, at best, ambiguous status, Barnes concludes that Ottilie's "holy love" does indeed conquer that other form of "magic," "the daemonic powers of fate" active in the novel (206).

at all times, "covered," as noted previously, "only by a glass lid" and artificially illuminated by an "eternally burning lamp" (VI:485). Its strangeness now recognizable to us thanks to Benjamin's critical illumination of an oddly similar nineteenth-century structure, Eduard's design makes the "heavenly" "arch" housing Ottilie a prototype or precursor of the profane consumer "arcade." The question—one that ultimately underlies the role of the architectonic throughout the novel—is why: not, as Eduard asks initially, "But shouldn't we build something more?" (to which we will return), but rather, with Ottilie dead, why should "we" build at all? Why construct a place for viewing an already inanimate body; *why add building to death?*

2. Benjamin's and Goethe's *Passagen*: Ottilie under Glass

THE STORY OF *Wahlverwandtschaften* entails, *as* story, the aesthetic objectification of those relations, the representation of the figural as image. Just as story and imaging take place within the context of architectural activity in this particular narrative, so the addition of building to death in the novel exceeds both its narrative and aesthetic scope. To pose the question of the concluding passage, and final building, in Goethe's novel—why add building to death?—is tantamount to asking what Benjamin saw, not in the narrative text he identified as bordering on the realm of aestheticized myth, but in the buildings he treated as if they were texts in that they were already aesthetic relics, the remaining *curiosités* of a myth of imperial capital, the Parisian *Passagen*.[14] The view of history that the *Passagen* housed for Benjamin can be seen to shed light on the architectural impulse

14. Cf. Susan Buck-Morss, *The Dialectics of Seeing*, p. 201: "In the Arcades project Benjamin himself practiced allegory against myth."

The reception of Benjamin's influential essay on the novel has issued, by contrast, in the widely held view of the *Wahlverwandtschaften* as being itself a work of "myth," a view blind to the contradiction between that simplifying characterization and Benjamin's own language-based critique of the subordination of the literary and the aesthetic—forms of representation constitutive of historical-epistemological objects—to either nonhistorical myth or an historicism equated with chronology. Sharf offers an interesting variant on this interpretive tendency, arguing that Goethe's novel combines "the social-historical" and the "mythical" in the figures of nobility who, occupying "a border region between Eros and Thanatos," "first develop in that realm into mythological figures," both "subordinated to" and "transcendent of" the "laws of time and space" (Scharf, *Goethes Ästhetik*, p. 218).

with which the novel begins *and* ends, as well as Benjamin's own, profoundly peculiar response to the *Wahlverwandtschaften*.[15]

Like Eduard's permanent installation of the dead body of "his life's happiness" in a showcase beneath an arch appearing to be no building but sky, the transparently roofed arcades enclose glass-fronted inanimate objects whose effect upon their viewer is to reverse, if not eradicate, conventional historical knowledge *and* knowledge of objects, the categorical differentiation between the given and the positioned, and subject and object, as between past and present, life and death (VI:485). Edifices that appear improbably to contain the external world, confusing the limits of imaged visual experience with the continuous act of movement through space, the arcades turn the natural view of the synecdochic relation of building to world, as of seeing to doing, inside out. Side-chapels for so many Ottilies, so many goods promising happiness, these historical temples of viewing create a public that consumes ocularly, i.e., without consuming.

But they also provide the medium for what Benjamin called the "reading" of "dialectical images," those whose "tension" renders

15. It is fair to say that the discussions in "Goethes *Wahlverwandtschaften*" devoted to the cognitive effect of Goethe's novel, in direct opposition to those that reflect upon the integral historical relationship of criticism and art, are rife with discursive qualities not only atypical, but even inimical to Benjamin's literary criticism and theoretical writing generally: tendentiousness, repetitiveness, and an unexamined conceptual assertiveness whose cumulative effect is more nearly melodramatic than critical, for instance, "The lovers are destroyed in as far as fate rules"; "Fate is the context of guilt of the living"; "The mythical is the content of this book"; "In such representations the sensory must become master; but punished through fate, that is, through moral nature" (Benjamin, "Goethes *Wahlverwandtschaften*," in *Illuminationen*, pp. 70, 75, 78, 81). The introduction of such fundamentally noncritical notions as "myth" and "fate" in Part I of the essay is accompanied by an equally uncharacteristic emphasis on *das Leben und Werk* of the author in Part II. Indeed, as Goethe is presented biographically, so is the novel—perplexingly—read by Benjamin *mimetically* (in the conventional rather than Benjaminian sense), as an unhappy love story driven by fate whose unfathomability resides in myth. See the continuation of this note in the Appendix.

them no longer discrete representations of history but rather "identical with the historical object" itself.[16] For Benjamin, that object presents past and present in a "constellation" whose perceptible but conceptually untenable simultaneity "explodes" the view of history as "continuum."[17] The temporally oblivious stroll through the architecture of the arcade includes the truly "objective" moment of its interruption, the moment in which history makes itself known in objects wearing *time*—their own time and another's—on their face.[18] Thus it is not so much the individual consumer as the fact of nonconsumption, of something preceding and succeeding us still, that passes its time in the arcade. In the body of an anonymous historical subject, a pedestrian pausing in a place of viewing that is equally a passageway, a space of traversal, the inanimate object of vision—"the historical object"—passes to the other side of the glass, goes for a walk in the mind of the living in order to come to itself.[19] The

16. Benjamin, *Passagenwerk*, I:578 [N 3, 1], I:595 [N 10a 3].

17. "Where thinking comes to a stand-still in a tension-filled constellation, there appears the dialectical image . . . It is identical with the historical object; it justifies its explosion out of the continuum of the passage of history" (*Passagenwerk*, I:595 [N 10a, 3]).

18. Benjamin, *Passagenwerk*, I: 577 [N 2 a, 3].

19. In an essay comparing Benjamin's understanding of the capitalist commodity and baroque allegorical object, Harald Steinhagen, by contrast, views this "facing" of the visual object as the unilateral "projection" of the "allegorist," the latter described by Steinhagen as a "radical nominalist" attributing "rational meanings" to things in the manner prescribed by Cartesian "method" (see Steinhagen, "Zu Walter Benjamins Begriff der Allegorie" pp. 670, 672). Before being remade by the allegorist into "bearers of meaning," the things of allegory "are mere appearance," Steinhagen argues, "in that they are transitory" (672). While Steinhagen credits this "projection" of meaning with the "interest" and "intensity" characteristic of an "emphatically tenacious truth claim," his understanding of "the subjective arbitrariness of the allegorist" underwrites an ultimately superficial or nominalist conception of allegory substantially at odds with Benjamin's view that the allegorical, "historical object" affects the cognitive status of its viewer, rather than only the reverse (678). Steinhagen instead arrives circularly at the possibility of such cognition by arguing that those same subjective "projections" that attribute meaning to oth-

idea—or allegory—may appear extravagant, but no more so than its theoretically imaged counterpart, Benjamin's notion of history encountered in the form of a "dialectic in stillstand," images that arrest the very dynamic of thought they reveal. In the *Passagen* it is precisely such an exchange of movement and stasis, of body and building, that is staged, with the result that history, as subject and as object of experience, is—in both senses of the word—"faced."

Thus it is also fitting and merely an apparent contradiction that the unrelenting, Eduard-like insistence of the narrative on the fact of Ottilie's visibility should have alarmed Benjamin, writing as Goethe's critic. In "Goethes *Wahlverwandtschaften*," his most extensive, and speculatively uneasy, essay, Benjamin describes the appearance of Ottilie in the novel as textually and cognitively disconcerting

erwise "valueless" objects come to take themselves as "inevitable" "cognitions" whose role *as* projections has "expired" (670). It is in this way that he links Benjamin's theory of allegorical criticism and cognition not only with the "nominalism" he takes to inform Cartesian method but with the "subjective" basis of the "hermeneutic procedure," by which "a first, subjective attribution of sense" is either "corrected" or understood as a preliminary, "virtual" "critique of the object" (670–71). This view of the allegorical method also underscores Steinhagen's understanding of the commodity as defined predominantly by its "price," an entirely nominal, always provisional attribute that cannot account for the supernatural attraction and power of the commodity examined by both Benjamin and Marx, nor the violence and "forced quality" of enactments of dismemberment in allegorical drama, by which, according to Benjamin, "apparently dead objects" [*scheinbar tote Dinge*] "win" "power over human life" [*über das Menschenleben . . . Macht* (*gewinnt*)] (676–77); (Benjamin, *Ursprung*, pp. 37, 113). It is rather the "dialectical apotheosis" of the baroque tragedy, its mortifying effect upon the viewer and "dialectical movement" between "extremes," that distinguishes it from "classical" tragedy for Benjamin (Benjamin, *Ursprung*, p. 139). Indeed, it is precisely her appearance "as mere appearance" (to use Steinhagen's words for allegory viewed nominally) that, impervious to such dialectical movement, makes the representation of Ottilie in *Die Wahlverwandtschaften* such an intractable problem for Benjamin. For, most unlike the corpse on the stage, or commodity in the arcade, Goethe's Ottilie is not meaning-bearing in any natural-historical sense. An appearance of beauty that remains impervious to the ruin of death, the person of Ottilie instead forecloses the "play of mourning" that enforces allegorical cognition, i.e., cognition that entails the transformation not of an object by a spectator

because it is just that, an appearance and nothing more, an appearance of nothing else. More image than person, Ottilie indeed appears most herself when painted on the side-chapel arch, as an ambient, two-dimensional figure lining a rising vault.[20] The literally superficial yet motivating presence of Ottilie moves even Benjamin to assume a most uncharacteristic, critical position: the same theorist who expanded the notion of *Bild* (image) to indicate the real or effective materiality of anything of potential historical and aesthetic significance—objects, images, gestures, lived experiences, places, memory formations, and all language, spoken and written—finds himself compelled by Ottilie's narrative depiction *as* a depiction to sound the alarm against the mixing of media. The transgression of meaningful aesthetic and literary limits that Goethe's particular representation of Ottilie effects will end, Benjamin predicts, in the replacement of the appearance of art by a wholly fictional reality, a world of appearances alone, much like Ottilie's own. "In the figure of Ottilie," Benjamin writes, "the limits of the epic and painting are crossed," with the result that, with any "step taken beyond Goethe" in the *Wahlverwandtschaften*, "German poetry" itself will "fall" out of the world of the "artwork" into the "madness" of being at "home" in an absolute "*Scheinwelt*" (world of [mere] appearances).[21] It is Ottilie *as* image,

---

but of the status and spirit of a spectator by an object, that, remnant of life already past, projects or injects itself into a present moment of vision.

20. Barnes makes the same point in describing the absence of mimetic detail in the "image-like representation" of Ottilie: "It is striking that in the, nearly exclusively image-like [*bildhafte*] representation of Ottilie, there is no immediate depiction of her so often mentioned physical beauty. The few details offered about her external appearance occur nearly accidentally and are purely functional: her beautiful hands (I, 7), her round face (I, 18), her long lashes (II, 6), and the color of her eyes (II, 13)" (Barnes, "Bildhafte Darstellung," p. 46).

21. "In fact the limits between epic and painting are crossed in the figure of Ottilie"; "If in (Hölderlin's) lyric it is the expressionless, in Goethe's it is beauty that approaches the limit of that which allows itself to be grasped in the artwork. That which stirs in one direction on the other side of this limit is the birth of madness, in the other it is a spell-like appearance. And in this German poetry dare take no step beyond Goethe without falling mercilessly

as "undisclosable," "speechless" "appearance" that prompts Benjamin, the most important twentieth-century thinker of the image in critical-verbal terms, to intone Cassandra-like against the concept and practice of confusing image and word, taking Lessing's caveat, that poetry that is like painting "binds the wings of fantasy" (*Laokoon* VIII), to its own negative limit, that of pictoral fantasy as a deathly ground to which the literary imagination plummets.[22] The repeated references in the novel to Ottilie's unspeaking beauty have the eerie effect, Benjamin warns, of making her appearance the "first and essential" fact of her "existence": in as much as "she," as a purported subject, relates to anyone in the novel, it is *as* an appearance, an image.[23] When, in the first cited entry in her *Tagebuch*, Ottilie

---

into a world of mere appearances" (Benjamin, "Goethes *Wahlverwandtschaften*," pp. 114, 117).

22. Benjamin, "Goethes *Wahlverwandtschaften*," pp. 130, 114, 113.

23. "In [Ottilie's existence] beauty remains the first and the essential thing" (Benjamin, "Goethes *Wahlverwandtschaften*," p. 114). It should be noted, however, that the novel includes its own partial explanation for Ottilie's image-like existence, her statement, after the death of Otto, that, having earlier overheard Charlotte lament her fate upon the death of her mother, she chose at that time to limit her movements to a prescribed "path" [*Bahn*], now transgressed: "But I have strayed from my path . . ." Yet this very disclosure, as Benjamin notes in another respect, appears after the major events of the narrative have transpired, which is to say, for the reader as well as the characters of the *Wahlverwandtschaften*, its relation of narrative motivation is ineffectual, after the fact. On Ottilie's explanation of her hitherto silent life as self-legislated, see my *The Imposition of Form*, pp. 131–34n82. It should also be noted that, in resuming her strict "path" of inaction and noncommunication after this speech, ceasing to eat and speak much as she had done before, Ottilie—responding once again to an inaccurate representation of her fate by Charlotte—dies without necessity (Eduard, *pace* Charlotte, manifests no regret at Otto's death), which is to say, for this most troubling of fictional characters, true to form.

Cf. Rainer Nägele's lucid discussion of Benjamin's rejection of the "totalization of *Schein* as the irreducible illusion of all human life" theorized by Nietzsche: "Benjamin's procedure is different: instead of totalization, he insists on the cutting insertion of difference within the sphere of appearance as well as around it. The work of art is not identical with appearance but stands in a differentiated relationship to it and within it" (Nägele, *Theater, Theory, Speculation*, p. 120). It is precisely the lack of differentiation "within" Ottilie's apsays as much of others, the *Scheinwelt* of Benjamin's premonition appears fully joined:

> One converses sometimes with a present person as with an image. He does not need to speak, to look at us, to occupy himself with us; we see him, we feel our relationship to him, indeed our relationship to him can even grow without his doing anything, without his feeling anything of the fact that he simply relates to us as an image. (VI:369)

In this observation, Goethe's Ottilie both precedes Benjamin and underscores Benjamin's point, and concomitant anxiety, about Goethe's Ottilie: a picture within the novel, she is also its very "center"; the "basic condition" of the narrative, she is a sine qua non without quiddity, lacking all particularity.[24] Just as, "exceeding anything that any painter had ever represented," she occasions an apparently endless series of secondary meanings within the novel—the *tableaux vivants* staged by the architect to mime other, recognizable images, and the "figures" of funerary reliquiae her own face transforms—Ottilie is represented in the narrative proper of the novel in a regressive rather than objective mode, in others' imagings of a "beautiful image" whose "full effect" they cannot "grasp."[25] It is

---

pearance, the totality of her image as image, and of its undifferentiated effect upon those "around it," that brings Goethe's text perilously close to nondialectical, mythic aestheticism for Benjamin, a prose rendering of myth whose central focus on a spell-binding figure of beauty suggests that figure is not indeed prosaic but, rather, self-immanent.

24. Benjamin, "Goethes *Wahlverwandtschaften*," pp. 113–14.

25. "Ottilie's form, figure, face, look exceeded anything that a painter had ever represented. A feeling connoisseur who saw this appearance would have feared that something might move; he would have been left worrying whether anything could so please him again. Unfortunately no one was there who was capable of grasping the full effect" (VI:404).

Cf. Jochen Hörisch's view of Ottilie not as image but "inimitable and uninterpretable sign," a "most beautiful" "allegory" of "poetry," in "'Die Himmelfahrt der bösen Lust,'" pp. 318. Hörisch's argument directly inverts Benjamin's by interpreting the imperviousness of Ottilie's beautiful appearance to meaningful interpretation as a sign of poetry itself.

these rebounding, inarticulate "relationships" (as Ottilie calls them) of image to image, of one mute surface to another, each including within itself, as yet another image, the seeing but incomprehending eye, which for Benjamin touch the limit of verbal art, not to mention the historical experience on which art hinges:

> For, unlike the muted language of the affects, this silencing of the moral voice cannot be grasped as a trait of individuality. It is no characteristic within the limits of human existence. With this silencing the distortion of the mere appearance has settled in the heart of the noblest being . . . All speechless clarity of action is mere appearance. . . .[26]

And thus it is also logical and no lapse of insight that the repeated fact of its being *seen*—a fact infinitely reiterated by its final residence within a self-reflecting vault for viewing—should make the centrality of Ottilie's beautiful appearance a kind of outer limit of the literary for the critic who defined images, in distinctly literary terms, as bearers of an ongoing historical life at odds with the limits of their historical content and chronology, a true if hidden afterlife revealed only in their interaction within a constructed field.[27] The *Passagen*

26. Benjamin, "Goethes *Wahlverwandtschaften*," p. 113. In his 1928 essay on Goethe, Benjamin ascribes this silent determination of the novel to "the magic forces of fate" [*magischer Schicksalskräfte*] whose end product is a "feudal society restored to its primordial state" [*in ihrem Urzustand restaurierte feudale Gesellschaft*] (Benjamin, *Gesammelte Schriften*, II:732). In substituting for the novel's own conceptually untenable focus upon the image of Ottilie the broad social-historical notion of its "thin but very incisive picture of the decline of the family in the ruling class of the period," Benjamin appears to retreat—perhaps under professional pressures—from his own insight into Goethe's representation of a surface allowing for no insight because concealing no depth, and of depth itself as a mere *Schein* "settled in the heart of the noblest being," embracing instead a historicist, indeed medievalist view of a simple, earlier society inexplicably, or "magic[ally]," renewed (ibid.).

27. Among Benjamin's many statements concerning criticism as the indispensable interaction of epistemology and history, akin only to translation in revealing the afterlife of the work, is the early definition of critique in relation to "truth content" in the essay on the *Wahlverwandtschaften*: "The following could easily appear as commentary, but is intended, however, as critique. Cri-

are at once housings, built to display objects to the wandering eye, and passages through which traveling bodies proceed. Both locational and dynamic in function, they are incontrovertibly spatial entities, neither narrative nor textual in form. Still, the already dated consumer goods they contain, remainders and reminders of past desires without immediate practical value, may have the power, Benjamin suggests, to enthrall the stroller's leisurely gaze. Arresting the motion of the eye as the body prepares to move on, the objects housed in the *Passagen* can make the passage of time itself appear present: representatives of prior, finite experience, these made things indicate

---

tique seeks the truth content of a work, commentary, its content" (Benjamin, *Illuminationen*, p. 63). Contemporary with the essay's acceptance for publication (by Hofmannsthal in *Neue deutsche Beiträge* 1924–25), Benjamin, writing to Floren Christian Rang (who had forwarded the essay to Hoffmansthal), defined "criticism" as "the representation of an idea," that is, the interpretive manifestation of the "specific historicity of works of art," in opposition to their historical contextualization, and thus internal dehistorization, by " 'art history' " (Letter to Forens Christian Rang, December 9, 1923).

An exemplary discussion of Benjamin's formulation in the *Wahlverwandtschaften* essay of the historically differentiated, yet intrinsic relation of criticism to art, is offered by Alexander Gelley in "Contexts of the Aesthetic in Walter Benjamin." Gelley does not discuss Benjamin's treatment of the novel for which his essay is named, including his unequivocal admonition to German poetry not to pursue the path to which Goethe's prose fiction leads—the path of the determining, yet meaningless, image from which one "falls" into "a world of mere appearances" as if into one's "home." Still, Gelley's incisive analysis of the theory of art criticism Benjamin formulates in the essay elucidates the urgency and meaning of Benjamin's apprehensions regarding *Die Wahlverwandtschaften*. For, as Gelley describes it, the essential historical relation of criticism to the aesthetic for Benjamin not only reveals the truth of Hegel's oft-cited dictum, that aesthetic meaningfulness, "in its highest determination, is, for us, something past" (see n34, this part), but also articulates the possibility that a meaningful perception of determined historical objects can be awakened in the present, a present in which, in addition, the aesthetic may "take on a performative valence," the "precondition," rather than foreclosure, of "politics" (934, 954). It is precisely this principle of the practical—historical, epistemological and political—significance of a critical perception of the aesthetic that Goethe's mythically motivated novel, in Benjamin's view, comes close to rendering inapplicable or, worse, gratuitous (934, 954).

and stand for a moment already past while at the same time providing the visual context for a present passage through space. At once medium and afterthought, they demarcate the trail of the present in the present, belying the self-identity of the moment like the shadow projected by the pedestrian's step. Like those figures, familiar from fairy tales, that spring from shelves and cubbyholes to speak and act among themselves as soon as the strange beings who keep them thus arranged quit the premises, the outdated objects housed in the glass-topped pavilions, the closed yet open pleasure-buildings that are the *Passagen*, may engage the passerby in a life freed from the spell of human oversight, the life of a secret, historical spirit lying in wait. Whether in the guise of toys or allegories, open to view or hidden under cover of the mundane, that life defies convention and custom no less than epistemological categorization, reigning over an exchange of time and space that habitual historical niches impede. In the perusal of useless things of uncertain origin and relation, something pertaining particularly to neither may pass between the subject and object of perception, disenchanting sensory experience from a spell of its own conceiving. In such a passage subject and object confront each other in the present not as antagonists but as each other's history.

The potentially "awakening," because temporally and intellectually unhinging, perception of the image in the context of the arcade, becomes instead, Benjamin avers, dangerously "spellbinding" in the context of a nonvisual, literary work.[28] A visually arresting perception of *verba* would render words nonsense without endowing them with the natural gravity and presence of *res*. Naming a verbally produced object "beauty" and installing it (verbally) for all to see, only raises the spell of the conceptual to a reification to the second degree, the making of an object out of the concept standing for an object. Words can *sound* beautiful, but in order to "appear" visually as such, they must stop being perceived, let alone read, as words, and viewed *objectively*, which is to say, as a meaningless series of shapes.[29] For

28. Benjamin, *Passagenwerk*, I:577 [N 21, 3]; "Goethe's *Wahlverwandtschaften*," p. 117.

29. Cf. Craig Dworkin's important, positive appraisal of the objective visuality of verbal media, in *Reading the Illegible*.

Goethe to have Ottilie inhabit the novel—before and after being "set aside" under glass in the "heavenly" "arch"—as a mute object whose all-determining beauty *appears* instead to stand for itself, is, for Benjamin, to come perilously close to falling out of the historical world of the word into a fully mystified world or "*Scheinwelt*," the replacement of words, by words, with a nonverbal world of necessarily pure or mere appearances. It is to join Ottilie in a painted paradise alongside Eduard and her many visitors.

For words can never, or only deceptively, purport to objectify. Yet this inability is precisely what they share with the made things displayed in the arcades. The contradictory combination of specificity and staging that makes these manufactured objects seem both keenly real and contingent also makes history appear present in them, objectively, here and now. In this these dated goods imitate what words "present" anytime and anywhere. Words, those enchanted human toys, can "shock" the subject into the "experience" of actual rather than chronological time, the present experience of history stored like the real good waiting to be redeemed in the arcades.[30] Yet words may do this, not by appearing to be something they are not—including and especially something called the "beautiful"—but by being, "objectively," nothing at all while maintaining their material identity across verbal and historical contexts; *always dated*, by definition, words occasion encounters with every imaginable content. The perverse usurpation of the particular potency of words by the narrative's repetitive verbal emphasis on the power of Ottilie's mere "appearance," juxtaposed with the discordant, non-narrative notes

30. Benjamin, "Über einige Motive bei Baudelaire," in *Illuminationen*, pp. 192–96. Cf. Gelley's observation of the imaged quality contained within the verbal, and verbal or discursive quality of the image, in Benjamin's notion of the dialectical image made present in the outdated commodity in the arcade: "The dialectical image, let us recall, is at once pictorial and linguistic and (one should add) phantasmatic. It denotes not only a potentially revelatory moment but functions as a label for the historiographic task that Benjamin set himself" (Gelley, "Contexts of the Aesthetic in Walter Benjamin," p. 952). It is this sensory embodiment of the "idea" of historical truth within the word that Benjamin likewise identifies as "the symbol" available at any "moment" "in the essence of the word" in his study of baroque tragedy: "The idea is some-

reproduced from her occult *Tagebuch*, effects a methodical separation in the novel of surface event from verbal depth, which is to say, with Benjamin, a fatal separation of perception from history. And it is just that separation that sets the novel in opposition to the verbal and visual works Benjamin most prized.

Together with Baudelaire's poetry, these works are the baroque "mourning plays" subjected to—and subject of—Benjamin's particular "natural" (rather than literary) "historical" view. In the history of the perceptual constitution—rather than historicist categorization—of the baroque this view describes, the momentary passage of beauty and permanent ruin of death are thrust together before the interpreting eye, contemplated with horror, insatiable curiosity, and commemorated in text.[31] In *Die Wahlverwandtschaften*, by contrast,

---

thing linguistic, that is, the moment in the essence of the word in which it is a symbol" (Benjamin, *Ursprung*, p. 18).

31. One could say that the *tableaux vivants* staged for entertainment in the novel are the antithetical twin of *Trauerspiele*, living *tableaux morts*. The physical staging and mute enactment of life's ruin in *Trauerspiele*, histories of life lived "for the sake of the corpse," and of "death" as the "form" rather than "end" of "life," are directly inverted in Goethe's discursive representation of Ottilie's silent, mirror-like beauty, which, whether viewed in *tableaux vivants* or in life lived *as if* in a *tableau*, effects the erasure in the image of any perceivable difference between life and its end *or* form (see Benjamin, *Ursprung*, pp. 95, 193–94). The indistinguishability of Ottilie's living body and perfectly life-like corpse suggests to Benjamin that Goethe has placed at the very core of his novel a mere appearance of life without end in sight. Cf. Benjamin's contrasting discussion of the cognitive and historical significance of the "speechlessness" of the baroque tragic hero and the "pantomime"-like quality of his spectacle, in *Ursprung*, esp. pp. 88–89, 99, 137.

Benjamin's perception of the ahistorical appearance of the image in *Die Wahlverwandtschaften* is, again, shared by Barnes, writing as a stylistic critic of the novel's representational prose: "In the image-like representations [of the novel], it is not possible to determine clearly the causal bases of Ottilie's return [to the castle]" (Barnes, "Bildhafte Darstellung," p. 51). Indeed, Barnes cites his own debt to Benjamin's "incontrovertible" argument in the *Wahlverwandtschaften* essay—that the " 'violently' " " 'material' " nature of Ottilie's presentation in the novel as " 'merely an appearance' " " 'crosses the boundaries between epic poetry and painting' "—at this point in his analysis (51n16).

an anti-baroque, anti-romantic drama is instead forever played out. Displaying beauty as always universal spirit and, more maddeningly still, identifying spirit with always apparent beauty, the drama staged in *Die Wahlverwandtschaften* is more precisely an anti-drama of timeless classicism, a deadly classicism as inimical to Hegelian dialectic as to Benjamin's dialectical images.[32] With Ottilie—in the indistinguishability of life and death that *is* her "image"—Goethe achieves, most shockingly, the representation of the "happiness" of the classical "life," the representation of a beautiful body onto *and beyond* death.[33] "Setting aside" the beautiful from the historical, while safeguarding

32. The representation of the atemporal effect of classical aesthetic form Goethe here achieves, at once enchanting and mortifying in its present and foreseeable impenetrability—the availability to vision and unavailability to change and disenchantment its entombment under glass ensures—offers a direct contrast to Gabrielle Bersier's provocative consideration of the novel as Goethe's intentional "parody" of romanticism (see Bersier, *Goethes Rätselparodie der Romantik*). Bersier interprets "Ottilie's apotheosis" by painting as evidence of Goethe's intention to parody romantic adoptions of sacred Christian imagery, just as the figure of the traveling architect with portfolio presents, in her view, Goethe's walking parody of the aesthetics, if not the person, of Friedrich Schlegel (52, 172–90, 164–65). Cf., by contrast, Comay's discussion of Benjamin's critique of the aesthetic of "Weimar classicism" as both requiring and exemplifying exactly the kind of visibility proffered in the *Wahlverwandtschaften*: "Vision falsely promises here to fulfill the ego's fantasy of an immanence that would elide the temporal gap or nonidentity at work in all experience" (Comay, "Materialist Mutations of the *Bilderverbot*," p. 353).

33. Gonthier-Louis Fink similarly notes the overtness of Goethe's "classical style" in the novel but attributes this to the "schematism," "extreme simplification and deep unity of action" represented in the narrative (see Fink, "Goethes 'Wahlverwandtschaften': Romanstruktur und Zeitaspekte," pp. 442, 483). To Fink's narratological observation it should be added that there may be no more effective and "schematic" "simplification" and "uni[fication] of action" than the conflation of life and death, and image and experience, that appears represented in pointedly visual rather than discursive terms in this particular novel. On the other hand, and complementary to the novel's emphasis on the visual as display, this account of a classicism based on unity of "action" must leave out of consideration the diverse and disunited architectural activities that constitute not so much the appearance as the context, and, more often than not, even the substance of its events.

its unchanging visibility, the novel's representation of the eternal classical divorces spirit from Benjamin's silent ruin, as from Hegel's silent symbol, so completely as to make even the foundational notion of the "idea" and its "representation," let alone that of art in its "highest determination," a thing of the past.[34] Preserving beauty, and nothing but beauty, *Die Wahlverwandtschaften* collapses the temporal semiotics of Hegelian aesthetics; preserving nothing but beauty *under glass*, it reverses the riddle of the meaning of art first posed by Hegel's indecipherable, symbolic pyramid, equating all we ever need to know of spirit with the phenomenal effect of a picture. In so doing, it not only defies the premise of meaningful form underlying Benjamin's critical apprehension of the novel as mere *Scheinwelt*, but makes the aesthetic itself meaningless, a body dead on arrival. The novel cancels the historical experience and significance of the aesthetic by making death and life each other's reflection, effacing the limits of transient, individual corporality by fixing it as image below and amid painted heavens, in an arcade whose sole commodity is a glimpse of that "pious body" (VI:488).[35] Who more apt than Benjamin, then, to identify the loss of all sense [*Wahnsinn*] to which Goethe's representation

34. The reference here is to Hegel's cryptic pronouncement in the opening of the *Aesthetics* (see G.W.F. Hegel, "Vorlesungen über die Ästhetik" in *Theorie Werkausgabe*, XIII:25). I offer a critique of the literal chronological understanding to which this, the most frequently quoted phrase from Hegel's *Aesthetics*—"Art is and remains for us, in its highest determination, a thing of the past—misleadingly lends itself in "From the Pyramids to Romantic Poetry," esp. pp. 344–51, 365–66.

On the philosophical "representation of ideas" and on "the idea as something linguistic," see Benjamin, *Ursprung*, 11, 18.

35. Whereas Scharf (*Goethes Ästhetik*, p. 227) argues that, "for the first time, in the *Wahlverwandtscaften*, death becomes the dominating power [in Goethe's genealogy of writing], a power that delimits the space of art produced in the novel," making "the text" "an absolute signifier" and "the concept of art that arises with it . . . absolute art" (for Scharf, the "art" of "mythical sacrificial ritual" that defines "the beginnings of the aesthetic in the west"), the critical perspective suggested by the question posed above, why add building to death, stems instead from the consideration of the anti-mythological, textual and architectural demarcation of place in the novel, one that delimits and locates death. The representation of the perceptibility of death, whether as beauty

of eternal mute beauty must lead. For the "limit" to which Goethe takes "German poetry" is indeed not Hölderlin's "expressionless" romanticism but an absolute and ever expressive classicism, a representation of representation forbidding mourning.[36]

BEARING ON ITS SURFACE her effigy and gaze, the arcades-like "apartment" in which death is made to resemble beauty at eternal rest may be considered, finally, Ottilie's own, the first and last the orphan child inhabits properly; or, just as properly, it may be considered heaven's built abode: the work of the architect has effectively made these two indistinguishable as well. Whether the confusion of heaven and earth caused by the vault's dual register of representation

---

displayed permanently under glass or as invisibility rendered temporarily legible by its housing under demarcated ground, renders death and text alike the near opposite of "an absolute signifier" (whatever that could be imagined to be in fiction). The distinct arts of *mimesis* and architecture, exhibited conjointly in the novel, similarly deflate any "concept of art" as "absolute," whether or not one views the absolute as originating in "mythical sacrificial ritutal."

36. Uwe Steiner's "Traurige Spiele—Spiel vor Traurigen" draws an important, direct contrast between Benjamin's view of mourning understood specifically as "play," and Carl Schmitt's view of "play" as "'scandal[ous]'" "'negation'" of the power of the "sovereign . . . to decide the case of the exception," a view in line with Schmitt's understanding of *Hamlet* as tragedy and *not Trauerspiel* (44). For Benjamin, as opposed to Schmitt, Steiner observes, it is exactly "the real condition of the exception . . . *which no earthly sovereign has the power to exclude*," that "determines that quintessence of the idea of the *Trauerspiel*" (44 [emphasis added]). Steiner thus reveals not only the fundamental contradiction between the political implications of Benjamin's literary theory and Schmitt's overt politicization of "tragedy," but also the anti-theoretical implications of the absence of any literary, or nonstransumptive, idea of representation from Schmitt's papist politicization of theology

See also Alessia Ricciardi's *The Ends of Mourning* for a timely discussion of the exhaustion and jettisoning of mourning that typify, in Ricciardi's view, the technology-based culture of postmodernity, as well as the re-emergence of the possibility of mourning such a loss may entail. Ricciardi's indication of a "certain critical postmodernity" may find its most enduring predecessor in the relationship both to mourning, and to the lack of it, so coolly, or classically, staged in Goethe's decidedly postclassical novel.

constitutes a prose version of Hölderlin's central definition of the aim of poetry—the making of an "architectonic of the heavens" out of words—remains as open to speculation as the novel's irony and the "character" of Ottilie herself.[37] What the novel demonstrates, however, is that architectural form alone makes that confusion—or irony—possible. For the viewers of Goethe's "heavenly child" (VI:484), her lifelike corpse displayed beneath the painted eyes of angels, no less than for the "building people" they least resemble, the Egyptians who, in Hegel's view, entomb their godlike dead within an impenetrable shape severing preserved, embalmed bodies forever from vision—for adherents of the visible and architects of invisibility alike, the housing of the purely material body permanently conveys spirit.[38]

Still, as a novel, *Die Wahlverwandtschaften* includes that formal truth within the purview of representation: the "images" of Ottilie's face (or "image of angels") surrounding her "ongoingly beautiful" (VI:488) body are accompanied by the images of a narrative that follows her even into her last residence, making that final "resting" place a stage for future activity. For, residents from near and far will continue to enter these "heavenly spaces" to view the fabled girl, just as it is in this "apartment" that Eduard gains permanent proximity to her body (VI:488). In closing, the narrative, ever true to itself, even hints at its own second-coming, Faust's fatal "beautiful moment" here transformed into the "friendly moment," "the lovers" will "awake together again" (VI:490). In *Die Wahlverwandtschaften*, Faust's purposefully "restless" pursuit of beauty meets its match in

37. See Hölderlin, Letter to Leo von Seckendorf, 12 March 1804, *Sämtliche Werke*, IV:437. I have treated the significance of this attribution of the architectonic to the heavens for Hölderlin's poetry as well as Benjamin's arcades project in, "Architectural History: Benjamin and Hölderlin."

38. Cf. Theodor Lockemann's complementary observation, in "Der Tod in Goethes 'Wahlverwandtschaften,'" that, to the eclipse of any "appropriate means" of "making present that which is removed from the earthly realm of perceptible," the "realism" of Goethe's novel limits its representation of death to that of "direct perception" (173). Indeed, one might add that, in this particular case of "realism," "direct perception" demands that death be and remain present among us, to cite the *Tagebuch*, "like a picture."

the body of a dead woman whose arrested "state" of beauty all acknowledge and want to see perdure (VI:488). If the mere utterance of the wish, "Linger a while, you are so beautiful," spells, by agreement, Faust's perdition, the "heaven" gained in *Die Wahlverwandtschaften* is the lingering over and lingering on of Ottilie's beauty, a heaven under glass.

The visible suspension of temporality put into place with her "glass cover" makes Ottilie's final physical depiction by the novel resemble her verbal depictions within the novel, that of a silent beauty now fixed forever *al fresco* from whose spell—so Benjamin's nightmare—no one wants to awake.[39] Yet it is not the novel's all too happy enactment of the deadline imposed on his bartered life by Faust (that exchanged life and the lovers' predicted afterlife being equally overtly fictive), but rather the very inertness of bodies allowed by the architect's activity to reside, in representable spatial relation, as if neighbors among neighbors, that demonstrates, in specifically earth-bound terms, the *überFaustian* capacities of all narrative representation: the narration of states of beauty and death *and* their imagined, ongoing cohabitation, "realist" description as well as myth and "pure" speculation. And because there is no eye poised above glass or heavenly ceiling, no external agency supervising what the architect does, the same must be the case for architectural activity, too. It is, after all, the particular representations of the narrative within which he acts that engage the architect, like the Hauptmann before him, to improve Eduard's grounds in the first place; and it is the narrative prominence granted the architect in the second place, or "Second Part," his stated "replacement" of the departed Eduard and Hauptmann, that, bringing him into greater contact with Charlotte and Ottilie, causes him to abandon the "plan" to convert the side chapel into a "memorial to earlier times and their tastes" through the painted reproduction of mourning memorabilia. It is these copied mementos and symbolizations of death, transported

39. Cf. Howard Caygill, *Walter Benjamin*, p. 50: "Benjamin predicts that the critic who would unveil the immortal truth behind its symbolic appearance will be defeated by Goethe's text, whose 'truth' is that the veil of appearances and the veiled truth cannot be separated from each other."

from their original aesthetic and temporal context, which the architect had displayed to his hostesses like a traveling "merchant of fashion":

> The architect could not omit to include the chapel immediately in his plan and especially to reproduce the narrow space as a memorial to earlier times and their tastes. He had already imagined to himself the empty surfaces decorated according to his inclination, and looked forward thereby to exercising his painterly talent. . . . Before all else, as promised, he showed the ladies different imitations and sketches of old grave monuments, urns and other neighboring things. . . . He had these so neatly and conveniently arranged into drawers and compartments, laid on specially cut boards covered with cloth . . . that one looked upon them with pleasure as upon the boxed goods of a fashion merchant. . . . They were for the most part of German origin . . . (VI:366–67)

Whatever the status of the heavenly imaged arch the architect paints instead, and of the corporal objects it houses—be they, Ottilie and Eduard, "holy" or all too human—these bodies and these images are no knock-off of once fashionable funerary bric-a-brac "of mostly German origin" [*meistenteils deutschen Urpsrungs*], no combination and reduction of *Reproduzierbarkeit* and *deutschen Trauerspiel* into kitsch (VI:367). If the narrative of *Die Wahlverwandtschaften*, in endlessly promulgating pure appearances, maddeningly prohibits the mourning of death, of the loss of the real, it also forestalls the inevitable use of representations of loss as disposable home decoration, the ornamentation, "according to one's inclination," of a world already built, a world in which the recorded state of the dead is a mere fashion statement for the living (VI:367).

3. Nature in Pieces

THE NOVEL'S OPENING architectural activities ultimately end by housing and displaying the appearance of beauty, along with its most ardent viewer, in a visitors' arcade. In that it "contains" the central experience narrated in the novel and echoed in its reception, this arched vault is truly a structure turned outside-in, an enclosing yet open exhibit that includes even Benjamin among its historical objects. Its paradoxical, if not impossible, effect is to stage the power of an appearance that no contextualizing architecture can limit, a specifically literary achievement of the very order with which Benjamin feared the novel had broken. For, whether living or dead, housed in one building or another, Ottilie's "undisclosable" image compels the forming and transforming of relations in the text. The perpetuation of those relations gives them the appearance of timelessness, of forces holding each other in place, just as they co-figure their offspring, Otto's, face. But this is an appearance whose illusory quality only brings the experience of history closer to the experience of the material in Benjamin's sense, the sudden experience of finding in one's arms not life but a corpse, not an imagined beloved but Otto's "hardened" body (VI:457).[40]

Performing a similar double duty, the architectural acts that lay out the visual surface of *Wahlverwandtschaften* also provide the catalyst for action in the novel. In direct contrast to the "tragedy" of

40. Described only as the visible image of the invisible imaginings at its conception, the brief life of baby Otto plays out the *Wahlverwandtschaften* it embodies as the ultimate *Trauerspiel manqué,* that of a life left *un*lived "for the sake of the corpse," Ottilie's true progeny.

Faust, *Die Wahlverwandtschaften*, pointedly subtitled "a novel," presents acts of building not as the climax of otherwise insatiable desire but in the complacent domestic light appropriate to its genre. Like the drafting and realization of the Hauptmann's "topographical map" (VI:266), building in the novel frames the actions and appearance of characters who themselves use the "frames" of building, its apertures, to view the world's "different images."[41] The room delimited by building in this novel thus acts like a *camera* both in the original and the image-producing sense, while architectonic renderings drawn for the purpose of building further make the familiar world seem "a new creation," and one's "possessions," even more "clearly" one's own: "Edward saw his possessions clearest on paper, brought forth like a new creation. He believed he was first becoming acquainted with them; they seemed only now truly to belong to him" (VI:261). Before there arises the erotic longing to possess and be possessed by another, to be nothing other than in relation, the clarity of the architectonic view of things in the novel yields a "new" relation not only to things but to oneself. In the comprehensive delineation of one's objects and grounds, one "first" sees oneself as the subject to whom they belong; by force of its mere graphic representation, the viewed effects in the viewer a heightened sense of self-possession, a traditional if entirely fictional progression to a new dialectical threshold, objective subjecthood.

41. "Charlotte received her husband at the door and had him sit in such a way that through the door and windows he could view in one glance the different images that showed the landscape as if in a frame" (VI:243). Konrad (*Goethes "Wahlverwandtschaften,"* p. 18) attributes this eclipse of nature by its architecturally composed imaging to the "architechtonic style" of the "early nineteenth-century English garden": "The distant landscape was shaped in conformity with the perspective of the glance." In "Das Motiv des Gartenraumes in Goethes Dichtung," Eva Höllinger, noting the "double meaning" of the word "Aussicht" ("view") in the novel, equates "every utterance about nature" in *Die Wahlverwandtschaften* with an expression of its speaker's "Weltanschauung" (pp. 191–92). Mentioning the *Wahlverwandtschaften* only briefly while discussing *Werther* and *Wilhelm Meister* as well as Goethe's lyric at some length, Höllinger does not note the impulse to "build more" to which all aspects of the landscape are subjected in the novel, suggesting instead that all "Goethe's garden spaces are essentially retrospective" (216).

And along with a dialectically internalized sense of possession comes the desire for increased, externally bound aesthetic pleasure. Whether by clearing or adding to the scene within which the characters are positioned, all building in the novel marks the creation of artificially enhanced vision, the fabrication of a new vantage point for a carefully delimited, "splendid view" (VI:242), the first of many synonymous phrases in the narrative for an aesthetically pleasing sight. The "pleasure building" for recreational outings will afford a beautiful outlook upon the natural space it commands once nature, too, has been artificially reordered, its given shapes, grounds, and summits sculpted to offer a more picturesque presentation to the eye.[42] Compared with the architectonic attempt to usurp divine verbal creation at the end of *Faust II*—the "act" of forcing a new foundation from "water" and the "blood" of human labor[43]—such acts of construction and reconstruction undertaken for the purpose of seeing pretty pictures at one's leisure appear inconsequential if not entirely trivial practices, as different as the playful effect of the beautiful from the violent experience of the sublime.

Yet the building of housing to facilitate occasional pastimes is finally not so far afield of Faust's attempt to rebuild the world from the bottom up: both seek to interrupt or reverse the force of time passing, to promote the "new" in such a way that temporality itself seems old. One could even say that a kind of quotidian sublime emerges from the confines of the novel's propertied settings. Much as the formal limits ascribed to perceptual knowledge and the perception of the beautiful by Kant set the stage for the internal transgression of those limits—and with it, the expansion of the subject's sense of self—in free action and the experience of the sublime, so the a priori forms of bourgeois life represented and embraced in *Die Wahlverwandtschaften* constitute the basis for protest that their perfect fit is too restrictive. The very first words spoken by Eduard to Charlotte complain, without specific object, of a general—one might say

42. Claudia Brosé helpfully notes that, in contrast to other works by Goethe in which artificial media for imaging feature gardens, "here the landscape itself is encircled as image" (see Brosé, "Park und Garten," p. 125).

43. Goethe, *Faust II*, V.11127, 11137: "*Faust I*, 1237.

"built-in"—sense of limitation that her finished project brings home: "'I must point out one thing,' he added, 'the hut appears to me somewhat too narrow.'" When Charlotte counters that the moss-hut is, in fact, "'spacious enough'" for the two of them, Eduard abruptly contradicts his initial remark, stating, "'also for a third,'" to which Charlotte replies just as rapidly, "'and also for a fourth'" (VI:243). As if to document the mind's self-transcending progression to the sublime, the perception of a narrowness of structure is immediately negated by incremental assertions of the capaciousness of its scope. Before the Hauptmann and Ottilie are named and the grounds for inviting them exposed, a sense of space is mentally measured and that measurement—*rather than the space*—found lacking, with the result that the real, as yet unknown quantity the space can contain is both provisionally designated abstractly, by number, and found to negate the discrete operation of quantification alone, number thus mysteriously building upon number, less than two becoming two, then three, then four.

Still, Charlotte reminds Eduard that they had removed to the estate out of a shared desire to live together alone. Having separated in the past, the couple, lately reunited, further set about to avoid any grounds for mutual discord. The success of their reunion thus owes to another form of separation, a voluntary division of their occupations and concerns. Calling to Goethe's reader's mind the primary organizational terms of empiricist philosophy, Charlotte recalls for Eduard the couple's agreement to divide their experience between "internal" and "external" domains: "'I took charge of the internal, you, the external and what extends into the whole'" (VI:246). Just as the categories of inside and outside, formed for understanding the unknown nature of experience theoretically, appear to stem here instead from the spatial realms of the estate, Eduard's question, as to whether the life they have literally built for themselves should be limited to its status quo, imposes upon experience the architectural imperative that serves as the present study's epigraph: "'The constructed site, that until now we have made our existence ("Dasein gemacht haben"), is of a good sort; *but should we build nothing further upon it, and should nothing further develop out of it?*'" (VI:247 [my emphasis]).

What is remarkable about Eduard's "rhetorical question" is not only that it follows from an equation of architectural form with the human mode of being on earth [*Dasein*] but that it suggests, without reason, there must be more such form.[44] "Build[ing]" as here named by Eduard is not merely a means of housing the living: both he and Charlotte agree their present circumstances can adequately accommodate the additions to the household they intend.[45] No means to a known end, and no instrument of a causally or narratively determined goal, building as represented in *Die Wahlverwandtschaften* is instead an activity with a life and consequences of its own. Before Eduard invites the Hauptmann, embraces Ottilie, and makes love to Charlotte in her stead, before the "inner" and "outer" manifestations of "chosen relations" come to appear inevitable by the mere fact of appearing at all, Eduard invites, indeed insists upon an activity having no internal or external, no reasonable or perceivable, basis for being: the act of building onto earthly being something more.

The consequences that "develop" from building viewed as an end—one might say, a thing—in itself, will ultimately include not only delectation but death. Accompanying the *Lustgebäude*, with its pleasing, unimpeded view of surrounding towns and countryside, comes the additional construction, from three artificially separated

44. Brosé recognizes the apparently causal relationship between architectural activity and story in the novel—"it is in the first place the landscape and occupation with it that evokes changes in the relations between people"—but concludes by conflating the two, interpreting "landscape" as a natural mirror of human passions: the "unconstrained nature of the landscape," Brosé argues, "corresponds to the unrestrained nature of uncontrolled passions" (Brosé, "Park und Garten," 128). While Brosé, nearly alone among critics of the novel, takes note of Eduard's question, she does not question its own causation, or the lack thereof, within the narrative, but simply restates its stated desire as non-sequitur, a matter of fact: "[Eduard] urges the transformation of existent circumstances" (125–26).

45. In *Figures of Identity*, Clark S. Muenzer also directs rare attention to the arisal of Eduard's question, but identifies its motivation with what he takes to be Eduard's and Charlotte's need "to reach beyond their enclosed world and invite others in" despite the couple's insistence that there is already room for four (77).

"ponds," of a "lake" *to be viewed from* that building (VI:303). The arrival of the "young architect" promotes the "transformation" of those disconnected bodies of water into a more "desirable," "unified" image, and it is beside the newly reconstructed lake that Ottilie will stroll holding both book and Otto (VI:332, 303, 454). Yet it is precisely the enlarged dimensions of this "water-space" and her inability to get "around" its expanse in a timely fashion, that persuade Ottilie to make her fateful "jump" into a vessel she cannot steady so as to reach without delay the "pleasure building" on the further shore (VI:456–7). If building allows us to extend our ocular command of nature, creating thereby a desire for ever greater objects of the eye's domain, it also misleads us into forgetting that such dominion is ocular alone.[46] As much as the act of reading beside it in which Ottilie "forgot time and hour" (VI:454), as much as Eduard's unexpected, impassioned appearance on its shore, the lake constructed to enhance the view from a "pleasure building" itself constructed for purposes of pleasurable viewing,[47] has the effect, conjoined with that building, of irreparably altering the course of events. Eduard may well call man "a true Narcissus," mirroring the world (VI:270), but the relationship of building to nature yields the world remade as narcissism's own deathly echo.[48]

46. "The sun had set and it was already twilight and the air damp around the lake. Ottilie stood confused and moved; she looked toward the mountain house and believed she saw Charlotte's white dress on the balcony. The way to it around the lake was long; she knew Charlotte's impatience to see the child. She sees the plane-trees across from her, only a space of water separates her from the path, which leads immediately up to the building. *So with her eyes, in her thoughts she is already there.* In the press of the moment, second thoughts about daring to go on the water with the child disappear . . . She jumps in the canoe . . ." (VI:456–67 [emphasis added]).

47. "One wanted to introduce above a pleasure building on the slope before a pleasant little wood; this was to have a relation to the castle; one was to overlook it from the castle windows, and from it castle and gardens could spread again" (VI:288).

48. That echo is indeed already evident in Eduard's version of the myth, whose terms he oddly reverses. In stating that "man . . . the true Narcissus . . . gladly mirrors himself everywhere, he lays himself like a reflective foil beneath the whole world" (VI:270), Eduard describes "man" not as "Narcissus" but as

This is how *Wahlverwandtschaften* begin long before their improper pairings are formed—not with love or desire for an other but with the desire for there *to be* something more, to see circumstances, the things that stand around one, change, to "build further" by substituting the new for what *is and has been* before. The act of rendering one's break with the past materially evident, so as to render it a matter of fact, is integral to envisioning such change itself. The Hauptmann, immediate beneficiary of the urge for expansion first expressed by Eduard, counsels that any architectonic treatment of the world must be flattening so as to be far-sighted, willing to "sacrifice" and "clear away" even the particular places in nature one holds dear:

> One feels one's way about in nature, one has a special liking for this or that little spot; one dares not clear away this or that obstacle, one is not audacious enough to sacrifice something; one cannot imagine in advance what should arise, one experiments, it works, it fails, one makes changes, changes perhaps what should be left alone, and leaves what one should change, and so it remains a piecework that pleases and excites, but does not satisfy. (VI:261)

In contrast to the topical practice of building as incomplete or unsatisfactory "piecework," the Hauptmann presents what appears at first glance a more thoroughgoing plan of attack. He recommends the removal of a "cliff-angle" from the mountainside in which the moss hut is located so as to enable, through the alteration of nature, the construction of a more aesthetically appealing path of ascent.[49] This architectonic transformation, or, in Marshall Berman's terms, "modernization" of nature, does more than simply replace the given

---

the mythic lake in which Narcissus sees himself mirrored. For Eduard, the "world" that "man" thus reflects is, at one and the same time, his own self-reflection, and the solution to the unfathomably "narcissistic" conundrum his version of the myth entails—attributed by Eduard, in yet another mirroring of man's narcissism, to his wife's misperception—will be Eduard's own personal mirror *and* worldly object of passionate attachment, Ottilie.

49. "'So would it obtain a prettily curved turning as a path of ascent'" (VI:262).

with the made; it exchanges the qualities of human and natural creation.[50] For what makes the cliff-hanging unappealing, according to the Hauptmann, is its own piecemeal composition: he esteems its natural formation "unseemly" "because it is made up of small parts" (VI:262). Yet it is just those parts or pieces he plans on utilizing to "build up" the path he envisions: the destruction of the cliff-hanging, the Hauptmann contends, would lay at one's disposal "superfluous stones" (VI:262). What the conception of a natural landscape composed of "superfluous stones" signifies in turn, is an understanding of nature that, architectonic to begin with, renders the very notion of organicism, of living nature defined by its own internal necessity, equally superfluous, obsolete.

Unhinged from their natural moorings, "stones" viewed as "superfluous" issue in a reverse avalanche of architectural activity in the narrative—not a cumulative falling down and away but a selective, intentional heightening and expansion. Even as the projected creation of a more aesthetically effective path gives rise to the suggestion that the moss hut be displaced "upwards," the "easier access to the heights" an improved path will ensure ensues in a plan to replace the modest hut itself with the more ambitious "pleasure building" (VI:288). Ultimately, even the site of this second building will be shifted skywards: in a comment embraced by Eduard, that "pierces" the Hauptmann's "soul," Ottilie suggests the new building occupy the "highest" point visible on the topographical map, thereby disturbing and "transforming" the Hauptmann's "carefully, cleanly drawn plan" (VI:295). From Charlotte, to Eduard, to the Hauptmann, to Ottilie; from building to building and from height to

50. See Berman, *All That Is Solid*; cf. Part One in this study, pp. 29, 40, 42. Rather than noting the way in which its re*place*ment of an organic by an architectonic conception of nature marks the novel from its beginning, Twardella interprets the representation of nature in the novel not as a destructive distortion of nature itself but as emblematic of the narrative's own pervasive utopian aspirations: "The world of *Wahlverwandtschaften* extends itself like an idyll before the eyes of the readers—harmony in the relationships between classes, sexes, and man and nature" ("Experimente im Treibhaus der Moderne," p. 446).

height: from the moment the world is put into architectonic perspective, drawn in two dimensions in imitation of three, building builds upon itself, displacing nature and itself without external limit. Not only our personal attachment to bits of nature but nature's own attachment to itself seems on this view to be just that, bits lying upon bits, "superfluous stones."

Architectonically conceived, nature can be analyzed, broken into constituent "parts" and rebuilt, its pieces set into more "satisfying" relationships in both an intellectual and an aesthetic sense. The stones of nature, revealed in their essential superfluity to each other by the same architectural imperative ("*should* one not build further") that proffers the grounds for the characters' relations with each other, thus remind us of other stones composing another, already humanized ground, a visible "piecework" assembled, bit by bit, of positioned stones alone. At the far end of the analytic-architectonic conception of the world first defined by the Hauptmann's critique of a nature in pieces, this is the composition in stone that Charlotte instead would clear, the patchwork of human memorials she judges not only an obstacle to aesthetic pleasure but superfluous to the act of memory itself. As viewed and articulated by the characters *and* narrator of the novel alike—represented, that is, as *appearing, from the first, architectonically*—the natural world of *Wahlverwandtschaften* resembles nothing so much as a demarcated artificial world, stones aligned to represent those no longer living in the world, a graveyard.

4. "Superfluous Stones"

IF THE HAUPTMANN'S EQUATION of nature with "superfluous stones" in the opening of Part One of the novel identifies the world of the novel as building material, from the ground up, the graveyard discussion that opens Part Two spells out the confluence between figural and architectonic relations enacted throughout the novel. The characters drawn into *Wahlverwandtschaften* have already parted when the second half of the novel begins, and the main actor to emerge with this turn of events, the narrator states, is the architect:

> In common life we often encounter that which in literature we attribute to the artistry of the poet, namely, that when main figures go away, or conceal themselves, or give themselves over to inactivity, a second, or third figure, until then hardly noticed, immediately takes their place, and, in that he exercises all his abilities in activity, he appears to us to be worthy of the same attention, and even praise. So, directly following the distancing of the Hauptmann and Eduard, the architect showed himself to be more significant every day, he upon whom the setting up and carrying out of so many undertakings alone depended . . . (VI:360)]

The comparison that serves to reintroduce and bring forward the architect at once reintroduces and underscores the irony of the novel's discursive artifice.[51] By implying its own identification with life,

51. Blessin and Gerhard Neumann view the complexly structured comparison of "common life" and "literature" at the opening of Part Two of the novel as indicative of deficiencies in the representational content of the second half of the narrative. Blessin attributes the emphasis on art and "poverty of action" throughout Part Two to "the historical movements of the age" (*Die Romane*

as *compared* with literature, even while identifying what we "attribute" to literary artistry with what we "encounter" commonly in life, the narrative exchanges, beyond all basis for recognition, the characteristics of the two realms it appears all the while to separate, making the novel, as it starts again, no more securely identifiable with the concepts of either "literature" or "life" than a coin nimbly passed between opposing but otherwise identical hands. In this high stakes crisscrossing of concepts, this "artistic" *or* life-like double-cross, it is architecture that serves as the constant to be passed around. By designating as the new main actor of events the "architect" mentioned only tangentially as overseer of the lake project in Part One ("*und hier kam ein junger Architekt* . . ." [VI:332]), the narrative makes the central *activity* of the first half of the novel into a *character* in Part Two, with the result that background or periphery and foreground or figure trade position and function. In personifying the "undertaking" of building as the indispensable agent of a plot for which building had previously (if without given reason) provided the ground or occasion, the first sentences of Part Two of the novel announce a transfer of architecture from the realm of action (of life like literature, in which the characters engage), to the realm of fiction (of life-like literature, in which an author brings forth action and names), back to the realm of action again.

The figural bonds of *Wahlverwandtschaften* have been joined and separated, the mappings, pleasure-building, lake, and park constructions have all been completed, and, along with a formerly minor

---

Goethes, p. 66), while Neumann interprets its opening sentence in particular as evidence of a narrator blocked by the "helplessness" into which the "main characters" had "fallen" by the end of Part One: "the awkward predicament of the narrator in relation to carrying out the narrative—now camouflaged as 'artifice'—brings about a whole series of efforts at framing which openly serve to 'focus' action that is drifting apart" (see Neumann, "Wunderliche Nachbarskinder" pp. 30–31). Neither Blessin nor Neumann notes the consistency with which art provides the context for action in the novel from the very beginning, nor perceives that the narrator aligns his story with "life" even as—by open use of the verbal artistry of simile—he here compares life with "artistry." Both critics thus effectively demonstrate the maddening circularity of such a comparison when posed within an artificial, fictional context, further confus-

character, called the "architect," a formerly extraneous activity having, however, everything to do with the basis of architecture takes center stage.[52] Already in the second chapter of Part One, Charlotte's clearing of the cemetery had also been mentioned in passing:

> "Let's take the shortest way!" said [Eduard] to his wife, and went down the path through the churchyard which he usually took pains to avoid. How amazed was he then as he found that Charlotte had also provided for feeling here. Sparing whenever possible the ancient monuments, she had managed to level and order everything in such a way, that it appeared a pleasant space over which the eye and the imagination gladly lingered. (VI:254)

Charlotte, we are informed dispassionately, has completed her own modernization project, clearing the graveyard of specific signs of the dead so as to please the living eye. With all of the complications that such an act of unmaking presents, she has displaced the memorials to the individuality of death that make a graveyard a graveyard, the spare, deictic texts naming and indicating those members of the "common life" we no longer "encounter," whether as a "main" or peripheral "figure," among the living. In so doing she transforms a place constructed on the basis, and for the purpose, of temporal differentiation—the earth-bound reading, in the present, of what has been before—into a temporally as well as literally "level" playing field for nonreferential "imagination." The narrator now describes in detail Charlotte's own earlier rendering of stones superfluous:

> We recall that change which Charlotte had undertaken regarding the churchyard. All the monuments were dislocated, taken from their place, and found their space at the wall, at the base of the

---

ing—in their attempt to oppose—life and art, or "action" and its "framing," and "main" and "secondary character," or actor and "architect."

52. Fittingly, it is again Solger, alone among reviewers and critics of the novel, who prizes, rather than deplores, the figure of the architect even as he accepts that figure's secondary status within the "tragedy" of the novel: "Above all I love only the architect. This is a wonderful figure, one of the highest perhaps in the entire work . . . I'd like to say he was too excellent to be the main hero of the tragedy" (Härtl, ed., *Eine Dokumentation*, p. 202).

> church. The rest of the space was leveled. Aside from a wide path that led to the church and past it to the little gate, all the rest was sown with different kinds of clover that turned green and blossomed most beautifully. The new graves were to be placed, according to a certain order, from the end to this point, but the space would be constantly reflattened and resown. No one could deny that this arrangement provided a lively and worthy view on Sunday and holiday visits to the church. (VI:361)

Replacing gravestones with flowering clover, Charlotte constructs a pleasing "view" unbroken by signs of any kind.[53] A color field artist working squarely in the abstract expressionist (or late Kantian) mode, Charlotte, however, has the added historical burden of having first to construct the canvas upon which she paints. In order to soak with color a plot of ground already marked for purposes of reflection, she must "displace," or "dislocate," from that ground all meaning-bearing "monuments" ("all the monuments were dislocated,

53. On Charlotte's aestheticization of the graveyard, cf. Michael Niedermeier, *Das Ende der Idylle*, p. 61: "Where it can be used as the motive for producing an elegiac mood in the shaping of the landscaping, Charlotte instead treats death on the estate in a purely aesthetic sense. She wishes to ban real death from her realm of life"; Bolz, "Ästhetisches Opfer," pp. 81–82: "Aestheticization is apotropaic. It is meant to protect the gaze of the living from the flesh, without signs of the dead . . . He who, like Charlotte, displaces gravestones, mobilizes the dead in order to call the scandal that they are to aesthetic order [. . . .] The dispute over the burial ground marks the transition of remembering from memorial to souvenir, to which aura is lent no longer by the here and now of ritual but by the aestheticization of form"; Richard Faber, "Parkleben," pp. 104, 125; and Hermann, *Die Todesproblematik*, pp. 109–17, in which Charlotte's "efforts at aestheticization" are compared with acts of "imaging" intended "to suppress a dead reality" (109, 117). In keeping with his interpretation of building in the novel as form of social renewal, Blessin, by contrast, somewhat wishfully regards Charlotte's "leveling" [*vergleichen*] of graves as a forward-looking rejection of traditional, class-bound social inequality [*sozialer Ungleichheit*], her physical expression of "the innovatory impulse of the principle of natural law" (Blessin, *Die Romane Goethes*, p. 68). Blessin fails to note the narrator's earlier observation that, rather than strictly egalitarian in impulse, Charlotte had instead "spared whenever possible the oldest monuments" (VI:254).

taken from their place"), the stones that, indicating at once the place of a buried referent and the pastness of the now invisible, temporal life they commemorate, provide the material and man-made foundations for earth-bound memory no less than abstract thought. Clearing away the uneven accretions of human life and death, Charlotte does not "return" the graveyard to its "natural" state, whatever that can now be imagined to have been, but rather produces an unnaturally flat surface upon which she may paint with nature's perennial, truly living colors. In "leveling" and "constantly reflattening" a piece of earth already set aside from other pieces of earth so as to contain delimited plots or pieces of ground, she makes the distinction between history and nature, including their historical ordering (nature first, history second), entirely manipulable, if not untenable.[54] Yet the semantic complexity entailed by Charlotte's purposefully de-signifying activity is precisely *not* based in an understanding of both nature and history as text. The undivided experience of the beautiful Charlotte would effect through the aestheticizing eradication of a deictic space of memorialization instead simply effaces from view the concretely textual nature of a place of contemplation, removing the

54. Intended or unintended, the practical effect of flattening a graveyard beyond recognition may be to efface the historical existence and identity not only of the dead therein buried but that of the larger communal place (town, city, state, nation, or "community" of nations) of which the graveyard, like the dead, are a part. From the point of view of those who knew, or even knew of, the dead, it is instead the place that would disfigure their death by erasing all trace of it, which is now irrevocably altered, buried or removed from experience, from all possible "revisiting": "How can I return to Lódz?" is the entirely realistic and unanswerable question posed of Claude Lanzmann by one of his interviewed subjects—daughter of survivors of the Lódz ghetto—upon learning of the plan to level the cemetery in which her grandparents, who did not survive the ghetto, lie buried (Lanzmann, *Shoah*). For this direct descendant of the dead, it is not the historical fact of intra-communal genocide enabled by architecture, the exclusion of the living from among the living and enclosure within a walled ghetto, but the plan to obliterate the earth-bound marks of the murdered that would make Lódz itself—a place in which killing was sanctioned and the deixis of the dead then destroyed as referent—into "Lódz," a mere citation of itself from which the substance had been vacated: a fiction rather than site of reference.

graven names and descriptions of those whose prior removal from life constitutes the ground of the graveyard. Like a dictionary of lost referents, a graveyard commemorates intangible subjects, marking these with the shorthand of technical, descriptive forms. Yet, *unlike* a dictionary, a graveyard not only *textualizes* but specifically *situates* its text in space: its signs at once indicate referents the reader cannot encounter, offering discursive in place of empirical knowledge, *and* they "mark the spot" where the lost referent is now placed, lodged for the mind's orientation in the world even as it is concealed from worldly view.

By removing the signs located in direct proximity to the subjects they memorialize—signs, erected for the living, of subjects already removed from among the living—*Charlotte instead makes death itself appear as death never is: merely conceptual*, entirely nonreferential, wholly immaterial, and thus eminently forgettable. A loss leaving no trace, this is death deleted as such, the past made truly past because cleared from both the surface and depth of experience, from perception as well as perceived representation, sensation as well as sensed signification. Irreversibly removed from present *and* future contemplation, history in the hands of Charlotte is not rewritten but unwritten: its graven signs upon the earth, of graves built beneath the earth, are displaced by the construction and maintenance of a seamless terrestrial surface, the achievement and afforded pleasure of a superficies unbroken by reflection—a *purely* spatial design.

Transposing and transforming gravestones into mere ballast and ornament, Charlotte de(-)signs the place of signs that are the signs of history, stones erected to designate and "stand for" bodies that no longer translate a living consciousness, signs that mark, as they take, the place of what remains of those bodies and those translations, memorializing individual experience by making its finitude visible. All this Charlotte removes, and all this, in small, is the fact of history writ large, the pure sign language of the dead joined by building to the real, the place in which the dead remain. The smooth aesthetic of Charlotte's design substitutes for these finite markings of the finite a single, uninterrupted plane. The adornment of that surface in continually flowering clover not only covers over the specific traces of interment but eliminates the possibility that the finite can be the grounds for infinite activity, the occasion for our awakening, at any moment, from the supposition of historical or territorial "distance" informing our ignorance of past experience—or of any experience whose occasion does not lie immediately before us—even as it reduces to mere decoration or filler the knowledge, whether new or commemorative, that such traces may convey. De-signed for purposes of pleasure alone, Charlotte's aestheticization of the graveyard makes the loss of historical knowledge itself appear—by its easy erasure—superfluous, her manipulation of gravestones and nature alike yielding a beauty that, at once artificial and natural, presents before our eyes, in delimited form, something like the death of death, the loss of loss itself.

So it is that Charlotte's aestheticism defines the aesthetic not only as universal but as universally ahistorical, incompatible with textual and natural history alike. Indeed, the pleasing nature of the ever-present view she constructs entrances even the church's resident priest, confirming Kant's view that aesthetic judgment is a secular "transcendental" act taking precedence over the personal interests of each of us, even and especially if that beauty takes insignificant, two-dimensional shape, just as Charlotte's redecoration of the churchyard resembles nothing so much as Kant's model of the beautiful, "wallpaper."[55] Yet, in addition to extending to sacred ground the characterlessness of beauty embodied in Ottilie—whose spellbinding appearance, unmarked by specific features, language, or history, appears "holy" in view of the individuation it lacks—Charlotte's removal of the gravestones also presages, in its effect on the priest in particular, the act of building determining the final Act of *Faust II.* Describing the priest, or "Geistliche[r]," as he regards Charlotte's artwork, the narrator uses the same pastoral terms Goethe employs to accentuate the destruction of the pastoral in *Faust.* "When resting under the old linden trees before the back door" of his abode, the priest, the narrator states, "is like Philomen with his Baucis" (VI:361).[56] From "under the old lindens," the priest overseeing the

55. Kant, *KU* B 49, X:146.

56. Goethe described his use of the names Philemon and Baucis within the context of the climactic land-reclamation project of *Faust II* as a means of calling attention to characters who might not otherwise stand out. The fact

churchyard Charlotte has transformed enjoys, "*like Philemon*," the kind of unimpeded view Faust violently desires, and whose realization in the drama condemns both lindens and Philomen to death:

> Faust: I wish that I possessed the lindens,
> The few trees not my own
> Spoil for me my possession of the world.
> There I wanted, in order to see far and wide around,
> To build structures from branch to branch,
> To open a wide path for one's gaze
> To see all that I have done,
> To overlook with one glance
> The masterpiece of the human spirit [. . .]
>
> So go and remove them for me!—
> You know the pretty property,
> That I chose for the old ones.
>
> Mephistopheles: We will bring them away and set them down,
> Before one can look around, they will stand again;
> After violence withstood
> A pretty stay makes good.
>
> [*Faust: Die Linden wünscht' ich mir zum Sitz,*
> *Die wenig Bäume, nicht mein eigen,*
> *Verderben mir den Weltbesitz.*
> *Dort wollt' ich, weit umherzuschauen,*
> *Von Ast zu Ast Gerüste bauen,*
> *Dem Blick eröffnen weite Bahn,*

(which Goethe does *not* mention) that those borrowed names already echo and invert their appearance, some twenty years earlier, in *Die Wahlverwandtschaften*, indicates both the close relationship of the two texts and the basis of that relationship in building: "My Philemon and Baucis have nothing to do with that famous couple of antiquity and the tale connected to them. I gave my couple those names simply in order to put the characters into relief. The persons and relations are similar, and similar names work there quite well." (*Gespräche mit Eckermann*, 6 Juni 1831, in Goethe, *Werke*, III:458).

Zu sehn, was alles ich getan,
Zu überschauen mit einem Blick
Des Menschengeistes Meisterstück [. . .]

So geht und schafft sie mir zur Seite!—
Das schöne Gütchen kennst du ja,
Das ich den Alten ausersah.
Mephistopheles: Man trägt sie fort und setzt sie nieder,
Eh' man sich umsieht, stehn sie wieder;
Nach überstandener Gewalt
Versöhnt ein schöner Aufenthalt.]

(*Faust II*, V.11240–48; 11275–81)

Pleasure in the beautiful and horror of the sublime share uncomfortably common ground in these texts, and that ground is specifically not given but built. As the habitation of Philemon and Baucis must be cleared from view if Faust's construction is to be made visible without interruption, captured in a single moment's glance, so Charlotte makes the world of the dead and their visible memorials into a space of purely aesthetic sensation by clearing the site of all markers of former life. Concretely enacting Faust's order to Mephistopheles, Charlotte, that least Mephistophelean of figures, physically "puts" these signs "aside" [*schafft sie . . . zur Seite*].[57] Those that have been relegated to the sidelines, "propped up" against the churchyard wall, are arranged into a chronological order ("*den Jahren nach*") that subordinates the disruption of death to a consecutive timeline; abstracted from the occupied place they defined, these stones now compose a portable calendar of death without referential function.

57. In the essay on the *Wahlverwandtschaften* he composed while he himself was set aside, interned in a German prison, Peter Suhrkamp calls special attention to Charlotte's self-appointed power [*eigenmächtig*] to clear the graveyard of all indications of graves, and the opposing wish of family members to indicate and make known the specific "place" of their relations in the earth precisely by way of marking those places with material, deictic forms: "each wishes the place designated [*den Ort bezeichnet*], where his own lies" (Suhrkamp, "Goethes 'Wahlverwandtschaften,'" p. 195). With considerable understatement, Suhrkamp notes Charlotte's "skepticism" regarding such historically held "values" (194).

The integrity of such a linear assemblage itself borders on the accidental, since some of the stones, the narrator notes in Part One, instead lie "inserted" in the wall, excluded from view, and still others are used as building materials to "augment" and "ornament" the base of the church.[58] Recycling bits of the physical news of the dead into the mere mortar of building, while "propping up" other such notices into marginalized side panels symbolizing the march of time, Charlotte not only makes of the ground an abstract expressionist tableau for the viewing pleasure of the living, but collapses the material-aesthetic bases—the curatorial "landmarks" and "touchstones"—of modern art history as well, effectively and arbitrarily leveling the difference, now in the manner of Warhol or Rauschenberg (and, before Rauschenberg, of the "ready-made") between properly disposable and properly exposable signs of the times. Still, unlike those art forms that, at once challenging art's abstraction as well as its figurality, make the stuff of history into their own content, Charlotte's double act of setting aside *and* re-using such materials serves the greater, antihistorical goal of more effectively separating the historical from the aesthetic. Her "modernization"—or destruction—of the graveyard completed, what the priest, the novel's Philemon, now sees from his doorstep is an unbroken floor covering, a colorful, formless, unified surface: "instead of irregularly shaped graves he saw a beautiful, colored carpet before him" (VI:361).

The graveyard has, in effect, become a room: its floor, a flowering "carpet"; its ceiling, the sky; its walls, floor-to-ceiling murals dating the progression, and overcoming, of history itself, artifacts and ornaments, of only passing philological interest, of who might have happened here and what might happened here, during the time before this room was built.[59] The effect of this transformation upon Charlotte's husband (and partner in husbandry) is physical, spontaneous:

58. "She had duly honored even the oldest stone. According to their dates they were placed against the wall, installed in it, or lodged in it in some other way; the high base of the church itself was thereby augmented and ornamented" (VI:254).

59. A direct inversion of Charlotte's project, effected recently in reality, is worth mentioning here if only better to convey the full impact and significance of what may at first appear, in Goethe's novel, a merely decorative—that is, "eternally feminine" *rather than* Faustian—undertaking on Charlotte's part.

"Edward felt a strange feeling of surprise as he entered [the graveyard's] narrow gateway" (VI:254). The destruction and transformation of the graveyard space into a kind of antifigural painting, a canvas cleared of meaning so as to be sown with color alone, is said to affect Eduard in the dramatically expressive manner more readily associated with climactic personal events. In *Die Wahlverwandtschaften* it is not the birth of a son, reported succinctly in Part Two, and from which, the narrative underscores, Eduard is instead absent, but the "coming into the world" of a new aesthetic field—here in the literal sense—that moves Eduard to react as follows: "he pressed Charlotte's hand, and a tear stood in his eye" (VI:254).[60] In Eduard's awed reaction to Charlotte's flat field steeped in wildflowers, Goethe represents to us less a distinct historical experience of French or English styles of landscape gardening[61] than the ahistorical power of a purely aesthetic moment—less Le Nôtre or William Kent than Monet's water lilies or Pollock's drip paintings.[62]

Yet, in addition to its immediate presentation of a new abstraction of the aesthetic to the eye, Eduard responds to the transformation of

---

The installation of a wall-to-wall field of grass growing in an otherwise empty room in lower Manhattan became a veritable pilgrimage site for urban dwellers in the 1990s: the mere sight of the room's contents, visible only from its threshold, reportedly brought about in its individual viewers a feeling of being renewed. In making a room for viewing instead out of the *outdoors*, Charlotte's clearing and leveling of a space built to bear the signs of history and open-air exhibition of its dislocated texts as if of wall-hung images, more ambitiously renders such a sense of the new (impossibly) nonhistorical—not natural but, rather, *like* nature, its earthen folds of time removed.

60. On Eduard's absence from the birth of Otto, see VI:420: "A son came happily into the world . . . Already during the arrangements for the marriage of her daughter, Charlotte had felt keenly the absence of her husband; now the father was not to be present at the birth of the son; he would not determine the name by which he would be called in the future."

61. Cf. Thadden, p. 220; Faber, p. 93.

62. Cf. the highly suggestive thesis that, contemporary to their schematization in *Kunstgeschichtliche Grundbegriffe* (1915), Wölfflin's conception of "tectonic," or "closed," and "atectonic," or "open," form, are embodied in the two parts of the novel, in Edith Aulhorn, "Der Aufbau" (orig. pub. 1918). See continuation of this note in the Appendix.

something that *had been no blank canvas to begin with*. His response thus also indicates this significant historic effect: whatever tears were shed in the churchyard till then, in the act of remembering or imagining what its gravestones indicated, Eduard's weeping, at the unexpected aesthetic effect of seeing those stones removed, quite erases and replaces them. The force of such a noncognitive experience is as incompatible with historical knowledge as the unevenness of the graves and specificity of their stone markers were incompatible with an "unbroken, beautiful carpet." Similar to the architect's disassembling of the "parts" of the cliff-hanging, here, too, stones are removed in order to construct a beautiful view. Instead of reconfiguring "pieces" of nature, however, Charlotte's project disposes of the forms already constituting a distinctly human, nonnatural world, the world of fixed placemarkers that supplement and instruct memory.

That world is the world of the dead as constructed for the living. It is the place in which dead and living, absent and present, meet in the minds of the living, a place set aside from all others to contain or house what has passed from physical immediacy into history. Essentially conversant or representational landscapes—one need not know the identity of a single deceased body buried in them to know, because of the signs they provide, that *somebody* is deceased and, as indicated, there buried—graveyards allow for a certain experience of time based on a certain experience of space.

5. "Stones for Thought"

SUCH AN EXPERIENCE of time requires the specification of location: for a grave to be understood as a grave, rather than mere ground, it must be marked; and for a graveyard to be recognized as such its own limits must be demarcated. The indication of a "here" not to be confused with "there" is what makes the apprehension of time on earth, the historical, possible. As discussed in the Introduction, in filming a simple enactment of just such deictic precision within the extensive verbal testimony and silent footage of *Shoah*, Claude Lanzmann achieves, with cinematic means, a recorded and thus repeatable demonstration of that fact. Contrary to those prescribed by the mason's speech, to be considered next, acts of deixis made apprehensible by the medium of documentary film-making need not be accompanied by the articulation of an enduring theoretical principle because the very fact of their enactment and recording define them and their viewing as already historical, *after the fact*. The documentary film commemorates—renders both immediately visible and historically past—the reality of a certain present, whether staged, discovered, or uncovered, for the future. Deixis represented with purely discursive means is, by contrast, merely an idea, and so must instead depart from a laying down of general principles in the first place.

Specific indication of place is the first rule of all building laid down by the "mason" (VI:299) at the laying of the foundation or groundstone of the pleasure-building. Taking place on Charlotte's birthday and intended to provide additional diversion for the living, the ceremonial laying of the groundstone appears in many ways to stand the principle of erecting a gravestone on its head. The unbridgeable difference between the two architectural acts would be the difference between life and death, yet the narrator indicates there is a familiar if "imperfect" way of translating between them. For the mason's discourse, related, like all else in the narrative, in prose, is stated to have been originally delivered in verse: "A cleanly attired mason, holding a trowel in one hand and a hammer in the other, gave a graceful speech in rhyme which we can only imperfectly reproduce in prose" (VI:299). The only poetry to which the novel refers, even as it "imperfectly reproduces" it in its own prosaic, representational mode, is verse explicating the general foundations of building at a ceremony in which a particular foundation is about to be laid.[63] Building in itself, the narrative appears to suggest, is a form whose irreproducible purpose lies quite apart from the unavoidably prosaic uses to which it is routinely—here, novelistically—put.

For, even in the world of prose discourse and prosaic purposes in which they come to us translated, the mason's words indicate there is nothing routine about the work he undertakes. In order for there to be building, he pronounces, there must first be an unprecedented act of reference, a founding definition of place:

> "Three things," he began, "are to be taken into account when building a building: that it stand on the right spot, that it be well grounded, and that it be carried out completely. The first of these is properly the matter of he who builds; for just as in the town only the prince and the commonweal can determine where [something] should be built, so in the country it is the privilege of the land owner to say: here should my dwelling stand and no place else." (VI:299–300)

With the "privilege" of property come the joint privileges of definition and deixis: the landowner says "here" and a specific location in space is identified, in distinction from all others, by an illocutionary act. And, like the "privilege" of property, of regarding pieces

63. The report that the mason's speech was given in verse the narrative itself can only reproduce in prose seems a less strange or self-limiting inclusion in the context of the novel's fiction in view of an early observation by Goethe. In a posthumously published essay on architecture, "Baukunst" (written 1795), Goethe equates the general failure to recognize architecture as "an art for itself," based in "intellectual principles," with an implicit inability to appre-

of space on earth as one's own, the act of indicating the single proper reference of an adverb is pure fiction. That indication will naturally vanish along with the fleeting presence of word and glance, if some marker is not made to memorialize it for every future present. Thus it is that the mason regards himself fully justified in "boldly" deeming that, when it comes to building, the "ground-laying" or "grounding" is "the main matter of the entire undertaking" (VI:300). Without the laying of a foundation *beneath* the ground, buildings remain vulnerable to the unpredictable vicissitudes of life *upon* the ground; the existence of a building that is *un*grounded, because it is not *under*grounded, would be only slightly more extensive, in the long view, than the momentary verbal reference that first designated its "right" location.

For the very same reason that the "grounding" of a building takes place underground, beneath the visible surface of the earth, this particular "matter" and the "invitation" to "witness" it are especially "serious" or "grave," the mason goes on to explain. Those present at the ground-laying are responsible for corroborating its defining act, the fixing and marking of a place through earthly engraving. They first exercise that responsibility through a kind of mental mimicry. For, as witnesses, they perceive and engrave in their own minds the translation from the intellectual to the material world and *back again*, by which an inanimate, self-identical object, a "stone" made to stand in reality and in conventional ceremony for an adverb ("here") is removed from view. Relating the "seriousness" or gravity of ground-laying to the "depths" in which it takes place, the mason describes the similarity between the "main matter" of building and "burying" as follows:[64]

---

hend poetry. There are those, Goethe states, "who would also like to turn everything in architecture into prose." See Goethe, "Baukunst 1795," XII:37.

64. In contrast to the seriousness specifically ascribed to such "celebratory activity" [*Feierlichkeit*] by the mason, Blessin emphasizes the "festive" atmosphere at the laying of the foundation stone (*Die Romane Goethes*, p. 61). Benjamin finds in each action taken toward the "completion" of the *Lusthaus* a closing in of "fate" ("*So rückt hier im Masse wie das Haus vollendet wird das*

> "It is a grave matter and our invitation is grave, for this celebratory activity is undertaken in the depths. Here within this narrow, dug-out space you show us the honor of appearing as witnesses to our secret business. Soon we will lay this well-hewn stone and soon these earthen walls, now decorated with beautiful and worthy persons, will no longer be accessible, they will be buried . . .
>
> "Even though now occurring under the open sky, the work of the mason," continued the speaker, "where not always hidden, takes place nonetheless for the sake of the hidden. The regular foundation will be buried, and even the walls, which we construct by day, are hardly thought of in the end." (VI:300–301)

The mason without whose activity the building could not come into being does not view his labor in terms of the living, all those who will "hardly think" later of the hewn foundation on which they stand. The basis, the "main matter" or "business" of building is not theirs to perceive or experience; it is its own business, secretive and obscure. Covered by earth so as to serve as foundation, the stone is "hidden," however, not only in effect but in principle: *basically—im Grunde genommen*—building "takes place," the mason states, "for the sake of the hidden." And although what lies buried "here" is only stone, the covering over of that occulted foundation, the curtain of earth lowered to separate it from the realm of the empirical, serves to reveal the invisible to the mind of the mason. As he reflects on his own role in this burial—the removal, or abstraction, of a material stone from view that makes it, at the same time, not just a stone but a foundation or "groundstone"—the mason asserts that, "more" than anyone, his being at "rights" with himself depends on his "making it right"; "more" than anyone's, his acts take their "origin" in "self-consciousness"; and, unlike anyone, he sees what appears concealed by seeing structurally, essentially. Even when the completed house is "covered over" with "ornamentation," "he still sees through all its external casings to the inside, "recognizing" therein the "carefully

Schicksal nah"), interpreting the laying of the foundation stone as "indicat[ing]" one of "so many steps of destruction" ("Goethes *Wahlverwandtschaften*," p. 76).

wrought," "regularly" interlocking "joints" to which "the house owes its existence and stability."[65]

In light of the mason's reflections—testimony to the significance of a soon-to-be-forgotten, founding act—the kinship between the gravity of building and graveyards, the "secret" of building, becomes, in part at least, available to thought. The *Grundstein* and its concomitant "joints" or seams may be the buried beginning of building, the hidden foundation and structure upon which the visible covering or skin of housing rests. Yet, as a form they most resemble the articulate structure buried at the end of living, the skeleton that remains under the ground, petrified by the ground, when a body that is subject to change has been removed from the surface of the earth. As the mason conceals the foundation, so the living bury the dead: one rights oneself in performing the task rightly; self-consciousness comes with the recognition of what one is doing; and the insubstantial shell of living is therein declared inessential, an effaceable ornament for the living to take pleasure in while its indispensable support remains, latent, like stone. The living, like housing, stand above the ground, happen to them what may; but the structure that permitted them to do so had

65. "In doing what he does, whom does it matter to more than the mason to make himself at rights in making it right? Who more than he has self-consciousness as proximate cause? When the house is completed, the floor leveled and plastered, the exterior covered with ornaments, he still sees through all shells to the inside and recognizes still those regular, carefully wrought joints, which the whole has to thank for its being and stability (or standing)" (VI:301).

One of the rare critics of the novel to refer, even briefly, to this remarkable speech, Thadden interprets it as referring not to building or burial at all but rather to the organization of the novel itself ("Only the mason . . . points to the symmetrical base structure of the novel, when . . . indicating the house to be erected") (Thadden, *Erzählen als Naturverhältnis*, p. 218).

Without referring directly to this passage, but just before recounting the course of architecturally related events in the novel, Suhrkamp offers the important ethical observation that, in every "place," the "duty" of the practical "activity" therein carried out "determines" "human life": "Everywhere, in every place, human life generally is determined through duty in the activity of a profession or trade" (Suhrkamp, "Goethes 'Wahlverwandtschaften,'" p. 197).

to be concealed from the light of day. The exposure, the revelation of that which gave them "being and solidity" would have spelled their demise. The essential must be concealed by the inessential for the inessential, the transitory, to thrive: why build, why bury if not for the sake of such concealment, "for the sake of the hidden," that which makes the housing of, the living in a body, possible?

And so it is no coincidence that the *Grundstein*, a foundation soon to be buried, is renamed and remade into a *Denkstein*, a memorial stone or, literally, a stone for thought. This "grounding" is no longer stone alone but a place made to preserve *memento mori*, to contain the present.[66] The beginning of a building, then, is marked in the same manner as the end of a life, in a witnessed concealment, within a "space" "dug out" of the earth, of that which underlies and upholds the visible. What the laying down of a stone, or a body, en-grave—in the masons' words—"'here,'" they exclude from the world of any number of "here"s, the infinite positions of experience in the world from which pleasant panoramas can be crafted like ornamental facades. Maps are made and landscapes altered on their face; buildings are raised to provide broad vistas, and nature, analyzed into discrete pieces, is rearranged: all this is building willed by and for the living. Yet, in foundation-laying and burying, the architecture of experience based in sensation—the housing of a living body by a built body, of one "shell" by another—finds its historical measure. And just as graves customarily bear some form of script to memorialize what cannot be seen, so can the foundation-stone be constructed to bear

66. Disregarding the mason's discourse on building, and the incumbent disappearance of the stone it signals, as well as the transitory, incidental nature of the things buried with it, Hartmut Böhme compares the groundstone become memorial stone with Eduard's "fetishization" of the monogrammed glass bearing his and Ottilie's (or, just as accurately, his own first and middle) initials and containers of objects of sacred significance: "the groundstone made into a 'memorial stone' . . . becomes a fetish that is meant to afford the house duration. To this extent the groundstone, like the glass, is a thing and a performative sign in one. This fusion makes it into a magical object . . . The groundstone, *from the outset*, is intended as such a fetish . . . as memorial stone it is construed as a reliquary" (Böhme, "'Kein wahrer Prophet,'" p. 103 [emphasis in text]).

beneath the ground information about those no longer living, a kind of burial in advance of the present for the sake of its future unearthing. The mason continues:

> "But just as he who does an evil deed must fear that, regardless of every defense, this deed will come to light, so must he, who secretly has done good, expect that this too, against his will, will be revealed. *For this reason we make this ground-stone at the same time into a memorial-stone.* Here in these differently hewn depressions different things should be installed as witnesses for a distant posterity. These sealed metal containers hold written messages; on these metal plates all sorts of remarkable things are engraved; in these pretty glass bottles we bury the best old wine, with the designation of its vintage; coins of different kinds are not lacking, minted this year: all this we have received through the generosity of our property owner. There is also still room if any guest and spectator feels inclined to bequeath something to posterity." (VI:301 [emphasis added])

If unearthed and brought to light *at a later date*, a *Grundstein* is indeed no longer a *Grundstein*. Subject to future action and understanding, it becomes instead a sign of the past, witness to what is no longer, including its own burial, its secrecy. First removed from the ground, it is then replaced in the ground and removed from view; removed from the ground again and restored to view, it completes a circuit that returns it to perception, but returns it changed. For while it itself may barely be altered, what is perceived on the basis of the stone, now forcibly unearthed, cannot be the same. Having been buried to provide a basis for building, a *Grundstein*, once brought to light "against one's will," serves as the basis of a kind of second sight, an object of reflection or *Denkstein* enduring the destruction of structures built upon the ground, a stone for thought. So it is that the grounding of a building is conceived to double as an historical exposition, a display case for objects outmoded not only at some "distant" date but as soon as they are thought of in relation to—and so instantly separated from—the present. Like the "buttons" a young officer at the ceremony proceeds to "cut" from his uniform and the "combs" female onlookers take from their hair, once removed from their quotidian settings perfectly unremarkable things become historical evidence: stored pell-mell, clasps severed on impulse and purposefully scripted metal engravings have an equal claim upon the "place" of the *Denkstein*. Just as thoughts of "posterity" level present distinctions in value, so each piece of the present removed and consigned to the future attains the status of a meaningful artifact in this *Schatzkammer* ("treasure vault").[67]

Like the showcase in which Ottilie's dead body is entombed, the double identity of the foundation-stone as historical exposition mirrors Benjamin's analysis of the displayed artifacts of the *Passagen*, but does so invertedly, as its reversed image, for this is a display positioned underground, in the fecund earth that encloses the dead. "'Here'"—to use again the mason's term—cycles of consumption follow the laws of chemistry rather than the alchemy of commodity fetishism, and, whether carefully worded or just cast away, the memorializing objects inserted in this subterranean room are immediately excluded from all vital currency. Unlike the *Passagen* and Ottilie's *postmortem* display, the buried installation of the *Grundstein/Denkstein* withdraws from the purview of the living what it contains, subjecting the visibility of its contents instead to *their* disappearance, to history.

Installed in the earth for posterior rather than contemporary experience, this grounding of building as memorial incurs, finally, the memorialization of building itself. For, while buildings house, protect, and so prolong the life of the senses, at the moment the buried basis of any building is revealed, that building—along with its founding "witnesses" and then future inhabitants—will already have been eradicated. The doubling of *Grundstein* as *Denkstein*, comprehending both building and death, life and its demise, links architecture directly to its inevitable visible destruction, and its own, long

67. "After a short pause, the fellow looked around himself, but as often happens in such cases, no one was prepared, everyone was taken by surprise, until finally a lively young officer began and said: 'If I am to contribute something that is not yet laid down in this treasure vault, then I must cut from my uniform a pair of buttons, which deserve just as well to go down to posterity.'

invisible, memorialization. The architecture that sets such a stone into the ground is architecture *and* architectural history at its origin. The stone it buries, having already been abstracted from the ground, is transformed from a conceptually "superfluous stone" into a foundation stone "hidden" from the living. An inessential "piece" of nature, displaced and dislocated from nature to perform as both material marker and structural, weight-bearing support, the "foundation stone," once concealed and forgotten, is, for that very reason, essential to the perception of human history: a "stone for thinking."

No sooner said than done; at which point many others had a similar idea. The ladies did not fail to lay their small hair combs inside . . ." (VI:301–2).

6. Kant's and Goethe's *Schatzkammer*: Buried Time

THE "PLACE" OF THE *Grundstein/Denkstein* unites space with time precisely by sealing that union off from present acts of perception. Space is everywhere perceivable, and its absence from perception, as Kant succinctly concluded (First Section of the Transcendental Aesthetic, *Critique of Pure Reason*) is inconceivable.[68] But time takes no phenomenal shape, and can be identified with no given body. Because the experience of time is not discretely sensuous, but rather inextricable from our sense of life and its negation, how one "views" time depends (always figuratively speaking) on one's differing "points of view," which is to say, on the unpredictable intersections of one's immediate and historical experience. If viewed instead in the abstract, as neither a category entirely void of experience nor a highly specific crossing of the general and the particular, time can take the *conceptual* form of temporality. The objective content, which makes such a formal quality conceivable, however, still can only be arrived at comparatively, through the observation of changing differences and similarities in the world. Such observation depends in turn on a means of denoting what is no longer, not yet, or not ever apparent: the conception of time as temporality requires, if it does not indeed cause, a recognizable way of representing absence, some indication of the lack, alteration, or termination of one presence in relation to another. The identity of those presences and absences may be fully or partly real, fully or partly imagined; it is their relationship in the mind that gives substanceless time the intellectual form of temporality.

68. Kant, *KrV* B 37–46, III:71–78.

Always here but never now, time "is" in "itself" unpresentable. Reflection upon it engages—if, again, it does not first produce—an artificial or imaginary world of representations, the creation, removal, and retrieval of aids of fantasy as well as memory. In as much as architecture can contain the conception of temporality through a marking and organization of space, time is the treasure buried in the *Schatzkammer* of this pleasure-building's—and every pleasure-building's—foundation, and if such secretive interment and preservation calls to mind Kant's famous description of the "true secrets" of the internal schema of time, which, unavailable, by definition, to objective deduction, must remain instead "an art hidden in the depth of the soul," that representational and conceptual resemblance is anything but an "historical" coincidence.[69] For, like the mason who, only "imperfectly" translated by the novel, is said to speak, unlike anyone else in the novel, in verse, Kant's openly obscure reference to the fathomless depths of the soul at the start of a work of critical philosophy aimed at clarifying, analyzing, and delimiting the relationship between the intellect and external sensory perceptions indicates that the internal basis for the "building" of reason he plans to articulate cannot and will not be revealed by it.[70]

In the mode of the mason plying his craft to the practical matter at hand, Kant produces an invisible but indispensable substructure for knowing what the senses bring to mind. He founds his work of internally coordinated articulation on a presupposed unity of space and time, the hypothetical synthesis of "a priori forms." As the basis of a structure of cognition assured in its own critical self-limitation, that hypothesis both makes the *Critique* possible and regrounds philosophy. Kant nonetheless attributes little value to such a foundation if it does not allow for the overthrow of the edifice built on it. As laid down in the ground-breaking Introduction to the First Critique, and unearthed in the Second, the "treasure" [*Schatz*] Kant would "bequeath to posterity" is an activity that the structure of applied cognition, based on formal synthesis, does not contain. Kant calls

69. Kant, *KrV*, B 181–82, III:190.
70. I have discussed this problem in "Architecture and Architectonics."

such action "free" (from the determinations of phenomenal knowledge) and *thus* "moral"—not an application of, or even a foundation for, but a "fact of reason". Such a "fact" can only be defined in turn by its unreasonable "practical" appearance, which is to say, with Kant, its occurrence as the "imposition" of a "pure," or entirely unlimited, praxis, and thus absolute homelessness, within the critical structure.[71] The twin of time, freedom is buried and memorialized everywhere in Kant's architectonic system.

Like Kant's founding hypothesis, and the "hidden" "secrets" to which it refers, the grounding of a building *beneath* the ground preserves as it conceals a formal synthesis: the synthesis embodied in the single form of the *Grundstein/Denkstein*, of the stone as spatially applied piece of nature and as hidden room and temporal container. The architecture erected upon that double foundation houses sensory experience but also marks the otherwise imperceptible spot in which joint spatial and temporal experience is lodged. In order for that underlying synthesis to be revealed, the architecture grounded upon it must be leveled. Yet the destruction or collapse of building upon the earth may or may not lead to an excavation of what lies beneath the earth: the spatial activity of unearthing depends in turn on one's temporal bias, the view toward an absent reality that orients and gives meaning to what one does. For if one views absent time archaeologically, as represented by historical artifacts, one might wish to pursue beneath the surface of the earth the remains of the *logos* of the *arche*, the "testimony" of a prior time that the downfall of a superficial structure can offer to view (VI:301). If one views absent time instead as a future waiting to unfold and wants only to build anew, it would depend on how carefully or ambitiously one's building obviated the need for memory, and, consequently, how deep beneath the surface of the earth the necessity of grounding would repeat itself, either disinterring or eliding history in the very act of looking forward.

But what if one's activity above the ground were anti-architectural as well as anti-archaeological; what if one cleared the stones that

71. See Kant, *KrV*, B xxiv, III:29–30; *KpV*, A 55–56, VI:141–42.

mark the place of past activity simply for the sake of present sensation, to enable an immediate aesthetic pleasure that any sign of history would impair; that any reminder of immediacy lost, of the *temporal* experience of space, would deform? This is precisely what Charlotte's "leveling of space" in the churchyard effects: like the clearing and repositioning of the stones of nature for the purpose of building in space, Charlotte's displacement of carved grave markers repositions artificial stones, but does so in order to *build space*, and space alone. In brief, Charlotte's aestheticizing activity is the destruction of Kant's synthetic a priori, the sundering of time and space whose unity in mental representation makes all objective experience, in Kant, a critical object of knowledge.[72] And it is also, at the same time, the destruction of the "historical object" such as is displayed in the space of the *Passagen*, the unity of temporality with materiality that gives rise to Benjamin's critique of history as progress.

In clearing away the stones of the dead as the stones of nature were cleared, in treating commemorative markers, too, as "superfluous," Charlotte effectively takes the architecturalization of nature pervading the novel to another "place" altogether. Concealing with a covering of flowers the places where we, as matter, remain, at once naturalizing architecture and unfixing the signs of memory by subordinating these to design, she causes the dead to be buried without a trace, which is to say, she buries language in its origin. And in so doing—in interrupting it—she reveals the relationship between language and architecture.

For, just as one who, grounding past appropriation through building, institutes reference and a referent where there had only been space, saying, "here should my residence stand and nowhere else"

72. The fact that Charlotte's transformation of the graveyard into an object of subjective pleasure most closely resembles the object and experience deduced in the Analytic of the Beautiful in Kant's *Third Critique* does not mitigate but rather underscores its destruction of the hypothetical synthesis of time and space in the *First Critique*. For Kant specifies that his *Third Critique* is the "mediating link" and "bridge" between the *First* and *Second Critique*, and that the beautiful is only one half of that mediation, the other being the violent cessation of pleasure in the experience of the sublime (Kant, *KU*, B VI; B XX, X:74, 83).

(VI:300), gravestones refer not so much to the individual historical life they name as to the place that has appropriated that life, its last residence. Charlotte's action results in the recognition that not only the landmarks of individual relations and memory, but the very possibility of relating language to experience depends on "designation of place," signs that indicate not "who," but "where." The churchyard's Philemon-like priest may see before him "a beautiful, colored carpet," but, the narrative continues:

> Still, regardless of this, many members of the community had already objected that, the designation of the place where their ancestors rested having been sublated, memory itself was, as it were, effaced; for the preserved monuments may well indicate who is buried, but not where he is buried, and *the Where is what actually matters*, as many claimed. (VI:361 [emphasis added])

Without the mental link the gravestones instate between name and ground, between sign and place, memory of experience would be removed from the real, and thus from memory itself. For the ability to remember experience depends on an actual experience of the present, the language- and object-laden world in which, in the present, the past is embedded. Lacking all relationship to material information, the nonsymbolic sense of "where" that clings to acts of indication, the abstract language and symbols of historical markings would appear to the mind mere shapes and itinerant citations, their words a fabulous wallpaper of free-floating, forgettable text just as gravestones themselves would become indistinguishable from their ornamental reproduction by the architect. Subtracting material specificity from memory, and confusing cause with effect, the architect deems the "individually" placed gravestones to have been "accidentally disseminated," and counsels their replacement by a single "enduring" "monument" to be "set up" independent of any one "place." In the architect's view, time clearly trumps space:

> ". . . one should not renounce memory, but only place. The architect, the sculptor are keenly interested in the fact that one expects from them, from their art, from their hand a duration of one's

being; and for that reason I would wish for well-conceived, well-executed monuments, not individually and accidentally disseminated, but set up at one place, where they can promise themselves duration." (VI:363–64)

If the experience of time could be consolidated in a single monumental figure, it would, of course, no longer be an experience of time at all; barring the moment of death (whether real or intimated), time does not occur to us in abbreviated form. According to the architect's "symbolic" logic, the irreducible individuality of temporal experience, viewed (correctly) as impermanent, is to be substituted for by a single pre-conceptualized, specifically nonexperiential place, with the result that the wish to symbolize time permanently reduces it to non-time, a sole unchanging object in space. The two-dimensional counterpart to this perverse, or rather impossible monumentalization of time—more impossible than the conception and execution of the pyramids, in that it conceals no body, indicates the presence of nothing different from it at its core—is an artful dissemination of indications freed from specific places, the beautiful here, and there, and there, usurping time in a myriad of meaningless, decorative forms. The architect continues:

> "Since even the pious and noble give up the privilege of resting in person in churches, let us at least set up there, or in beautiful galleries around our burial places, memorials and inscriptions. There are a thousand forms in which these can be written, and a thousand ornaments with which they can be decorated." (VI:364)

The removal of deictic markers from linguistic memorialization not only destroys memory's specific, temporally altered grounds; it disfigures language by figuring it in its entirety, making the nonreferential words it leaves behind into multiple tableaux of a timeless memorial to time. In this fully aesthetic scheme, symbol (sculptural monument) and signs (decorative texts) complement each other in their equal disassociation from the real.

For those who protest the gravestones' removal, that reality is not the stones themselves, but the "person" whose invisible proximity each "stone" indicates in the "present." The community members make their grievance clear: "'But it is not this stone that attracts us; rather it is that which is contained beneath it, that which is entrusted to the earth beside it. We speak here [or, 'the issue here is' (*Es ist . . . die Rede*)] not so much of memorialization as *of the person himself*, not so much of memory as *of the present*.'" (VI:362 [emphasis added]).

The architect has joined Charlotte in undoing the "present" effect of architecture, the knowledge granted by a gravestone placed above the ground—like that occasioned by a foundation/memorial stone placed beneath a building's ground—that something specific, a "place," corporal or spatial, of past activity, is indicated. In life and in death housing and foundation/memorial stone exchange "places," the one visible when the other is buried, each intermittently exposed to, or hidden from, the light of day. But marked graves and grounded housings are equally built phenomena, and it is these phenomena that the architect, now filling the mimetic role of "main figure" in the novel's plot, and Charlotte, introduced as a main character in the very act of building, would now take away, giving pure figuration full, if meaningless, sway.

Yet in so doing they show that such architecture extends the possibility of linguistic meaning in the first place. By constructing a basis for deixis, building provides the *non*linguistic grounds for both literal and figurative reference, a marker of "where" without a proper name of its own, and so twice named: foundation and memorial stone.[73] This "where" cohabits time with "what" even when the acts so indicated have long ceased to be apparent, their agency become solely an object of memory, unattached to a perceptible body. Establishing both a foundation for acts of semiosis that is itself unavailable to the senses and a context for acts of memorialization, the marking of the unavailability of the sensory, building not only grounds language: it houses language at its origin. Its destruction thus also takes

73. Jang-Hyok An refers briefly to the "gravestone" as a "signifier" capable only of indicating "'where,'" but it is precisely this "where," the situation within the earth of what remains of those no longer living upon the earth, that is at issue for the "community"; (see An, *Goethes "Wahlverwandtschaften" und das Andere der Vernunft* p. 196).

purely spatial and figural conceptions of the world to their nonlinguistic limit: both the architect and Charlotte agree that, in addition to a graveyard made a living color field by virtue of being emptied of gravestones, the "most beautiful monument" to the dead "remain" their "own images" (VI:365), and it is this violently aestheticizing, anti-temporal arresting of both human life and memory that the glass-enclosed corpses of Ottilie and Eduard embody eerily in the novel's final scene.

They do so, however, only from within the structure of a vault: these embodiments of the image are housed in another veritable *Schatzkammer.* Unlike the monumentalization of time and erasure of indications of place, and so of language, to which the architect and Charlotte aspire, the transparent enshrinement of Ottilie and Eduard, in housing corporal beauty and its adoration, displays the history and mortal consequences of sensuous experience, too. That history is the story of *Wahlverwandtschaften*, of the formation and sundering of impassioned relationships that appear to obviate temporality.[74] "The intervening time fell into oblivion" [*die Zwischenzeit war ins Vergessen gefallen*] is the narrative's way of describing a story with a singularly ahistorical effect, one in which the occasion of mere proximity clears away the need for any marker of "Where": "Only the closest proximity could calm them, but could also fully calm them, and this proximity was enough; there was no need for a glance, a word, a gesture, a touch: only for pure being together" (VI:478). Thus the architecture that, without narrated ground or motive, propels the story and formation of *Wahlverwandtschaften* in this novel, is the same that provides the artificial grounds for reference *and* figuration, that marks the spot not only of the birth of language, but of its death or suspension in the sensory embrace of the beautiful. And, in this,

74. In *Zeitstrukturen in Goethes "Wahlverwandtschaften,"* Judith Reusch perceptively describes the absence of temporal awareness demonstrated in the novel but fails to note the dependence of such a "timeless space" and "context" on the enclosed spaces of co-presence and contiguity brought about in it by acts of building: "Through the lack of the sense of time a deceptive, timeless space is created . . . The characters of the novel move in a context robbed of every feeling of time" (11).

it draws the very line "where," echoing both Benjamin and Faust, language and the beautiful cross, into time.

The community may well say, "But it is not this stone that attracts us . . . we speak not of memorialization but of the person, not of memory, but of the present." Yet, the positing of the stone as marker, indicating "that which is contained beneath it," *is* indeed that which, even without inscription, brings the past into the "present." Stones, pieces of nature, are anything but "superfluous" when indicating what remains of the absent "person" "contained under them," the presence no longer proximate to the living. Stones that alternately house the living and indicate to the living the present reality of the dead are the ground and memorial, the matter and mark, that together transcribe time, its perceived presence and perceived absence, into space. In Goethe's novel, that transcription is not a suspension of temporality by the spatial. Nor is it the purely formal, theoretical synthesis of the two. It is the link between life on earth and earth, the language that articulates space for the living, that asks, "where," and indicates, "here" and not someplace else: that lays the foundation for history, including the possibility of future historical knowledge, and then buries it; and, it is built.

AFTERWORD

Gravity: Metaphysics of the Referent

"GRAVE" IS AN especially polysemous, formally versatile word in English, whose history of multiple meanings and grammatical functions betrays an unusually dense nexus or set of concepts when compared with the lexical differentiation of these in related, and relatively less hybrid, modern languages. Locative (dative case) descendant of the Old English *graf* or *graff* deriving from *grafan*, "to dig," "grave" in Middle English designated the location of a specific object of digging, a "place of burial," the name of an action, in the form of a transitive verb, attributed to the end of that action, in the form of a substantive.[1] By the thirteenth century, the nominal meaning of "grave" had extended significantly, from that of the particular piece of ground set aside for "the reception of a corpse" to any portion of ground instead appropriated by and passed on to the living. Spanning the substantive and categorical gaps between place and person, and past and present, this powerful, metonymic development encompassed both the particular plot of earth appropriated for the dead and "any person put in charge of property" (thus "landgrave," "margrave," and the foreign language, *Graf*, or "count") in its range of meaning.

In the fourteenth and fifteenth centuries, that semantic field expanded further into another register, as the physical—spatial or human—"grave" was figuratively equated in popular and proverbial expressions with the essential definition ("turning in one's grave"), end ("one foot in the grave"), or incommunicability ("secret as a grave") of the individual life. In pastoral, hymnal, and elegiac verse from Wycliffe through Gray, Wordsworth, and Shelley, "grave" came to stand

1. The senses of "grave" delineated in the following discussion are based both on primary texts and the textual evidence marshaled in the OED.

not for the defining limit of life but for its opposite, the general "state or condition of being dead," or incumbent fact of "death," linked to the experiences of living, if at all, by an adverbial prefix or postverbal marker of negation (Wordsworth, *The Prelude*, Bk. I, l.267: "Unprofitably traveling toward the grave"; Shelley, "Preface to *Alastor*: "he descends to an untimely grave" and "Those who love not their fellow-beings live unfruitful lives, and prepare for their old age a miserable grave"; *Alastor*, l.720: "Birth and the grave, that are not as they were"). Still in the fourteenth century, "grave" was used, in addition, to mean the artificial intersection of the living and the dead, the concrete representation, present to the living, of something no longer present but formally perfected: "the graven image."

While its nominal meanings developed, "grave" continued to change as a verb. Its limited earlier meaning, "dig"—literally expanded, in the eleventh century, to mean "dig out," or "excavate"—included the notion of excavation both as historical uncovering and aesthetic formation, the partial removal of matter signified by "carve" and "engrave." The placement of a body taking the place of the earth it displaces, and the artificial production of space as meaningful form appear the reversed or negative images of a single activity, as "grave" came to signify, in the thirteenth century, both "bury," or "deposit in the ground," and "record by engraved or incised letters." Personalizing the matter thus set aside and the identity so inscribed, Chaucer, in *Troylus and Cressida*, like Shakespeare in *Venus and Adonis*, used "grave" to mean "mark by incision" and "ornament with incised marks" when referring to the recalcitrance—"hard[ness]" or "steele"—of the lover's "heart." While Sidney and Locke followed Gower in using "grave" to mean to mark so as to "impress" or "fix indelibly," it was, appropriately, Donne who signaled the transition of the verb into the more fluid activity of transcription. In Donne's Sermons, "grave" indicates the production not of a single mark or image but the always potentially multiple "copy," a reproduction that, based upon engraving, an incising below or inside the surface, allows the transportation of the engraved, at any time and place, from one surface of meaning to another.

In keeping with this new, more general sense of transcription, the OED relates the Old English *grafan*, "to dig, to engrave," and *begrafen*, "to bury," along with *graf* and its alternate form *graff*—sixteenth century verbal forms for "insert," "set or fix firmly"—to both "spade" for digging and "graft, scion, or *greffe*." Yet, even as it notes that the connection between spade and scion was "suggested by the similarity of [their] shape" to that of a third term and etymological stem, that of the *graffe*, "stylus or pen," derived from the Greek *graphein*, in Old French, the OED offers, without further explanation, that, among the verbal senses of "grave," "its connection with the Greek γράφειν, to write, is no longer accepted by philologists."[2] That connection, however, was presumably accepted a century and a half earlier when Keats wrote the following lines closing the preamble stanza of *The Fall of Hyperion* (l.16–18): "Whether the dream now purposed to rehearse / Be poet's or fanatic's will be known / When this warm scribe my hand is in the grave."

In addition to its usage as a noun and a verb, "grave" later acquired the function of an adjective. Since the mid-sixteenth century, it has described the concrete condition of "having weight." A series of figural descriptive meanings ascribed to nominative subjects were derived from that empirical state: "weighty, of importance, influential, respected," as related to "persons"; "weighty, authoritative," as related to "authors, books, maxims, advice" as well as "works, employment, objects of consideration"; and, beginning in the nineteenth century, any matter "requiring serious thought." Toward the close of the sixteenth century, "grave" was used to indicate "solemnity" or "seriousness" of "movements," "music," and "tones of voice," and, in the seventeenth century, "dull, plain" and "somber" "color and dress," as well as "low in pitch, deep in tone" with regard to "musical notes." Finally, in usage by Chapman through Wordsworth, "grave"

2. Regardless of whether one follows the recent judgment of the editors of the OED (1972 ed.) or that of the earlier philologists it notes, and relates "grave" (from *grafan*), in its verbal form, with "graft" (from the Old French "graffe" or stylus) and the graphic act of "writing" (from *graphein*), it remains worth noting, in the present context, that the first sentence of Goethe's novel joins its own initial act of "naming" a character with that character's initial, "just completed" act of incising or "grafting": "Edward—so let us name a rich baron in the best years of his life—Edward had spent the most beautiful hour of an April afternoon in his arboretum, in order to place a newly gathered graft on young stems. His business was just completed [or perfected: *vollendet*] . . ." (VI:242).

also closely followed the Latin *gravis* to mean, usually of an object, "physically ponderous, heavy."

Although German employs the same word stem to indicate the substantive, "grave" (*Grab*), and the verbs, "grave," or "bury" (*eingraben*), and "engrave" (*eingravieren*), it uses other stems for the adjectival meanings that English, in reflecting its Latin roots, ascribes to "grave," even while English maintains its Germanic roots in its synonyms for the same: "weighty" (*gewichtig*) and "deep" (*tief*), "serious" or "earnest" (*ernst*).[3] While romance languages maintain these adjectival senses of "grave," and the verbal sense of "grave" as "engrave" (*graver*; *gravar*), they employ a form of "tomb" (*tombeau*, *tomba*, *tumba*), derived solely from the Latin *tumulus*, for the substantive, "grave," and similarly separate the senses of having weight, depth, or seriousness from the act of burying, which they signify concretely as the "setting into the earth" derived again solely from a compound of Latin terms (*enterrer*, *enterrar*, *sottoterrare*) itself reflected in the synonymous English romance derivative, "inter."

The complex development of "grave" in English, coincident with its wide semantic array, has also contributed to the ambiguity of the English word "gravity." The OED describes that double meaning as staggered, descriptive and figural before it is constative and physical, noting that, "first introduced in its figural senses, corresponding generally to the English senses of the adjective," "gravity," understood as "grave, weighty, and serious," preceded the introduction into English in the seventeenth century of "the quality of having weight" and "the tendency to downward motion" that compose "the primary Latin sense of the word."[4] While the German name for "gravity" is "force of weight" (*Schwerkraft*), and romance languages indicate the

3. In translating the word "ernst," used in the mason's speech, as both "serious" and "grave," this study noted and made use of the synonymity of the two in English.

4. Contemporary with the adoption in English of "gravity" in the physical sense of downward-tending, Descartes' early treatise, *Le Monde* (posthumously pub. 1664), employed a different term, *pesanteur*, to designate the weight of the earth-bound, thereby underscoring the continuing differentiation of the physical and figurative, scientific and literary meanings of "grave" and "gravity" in modern languages, other than English, that derive from Latin.

replacement or supplementation of ancient physics by Newton's general law of the attraction of matter (*Principia*, 1686) in designating physical "gravity" as the "force of attraction" or "law of weight" and employing "gravity" (*gravité*, *gravitá*, *gravidad*) in its figural, intellectual sense alone, English confuses the intellectual with the physical, suggesting that there is something serious about being pulled and held to the earth.

The seriousness that is "gravity" and the seriousness of "gravity"—the identification of these two, in English, by a single word—may stem from the very seriousness, if not the secrecy, of the "grave." In translating *gravis* (weighty) together with *grafan* (dig), the lexical history of the English "grave" provides a fuller historical perspective upon "gravity." That history not only combines a substantive, the place of burial, with verbs denoting acts of excavation and burial, as well as the appropriation, formation, and marking of a place, but conjoins all these with the adjectival qualities of seriousness, weight, and depth. "Gravity," the force that holds things to surfaces, holds them in, or lets them, or makes them take place—the purely physical force that enables life on the surface, life *on* earth to take place—is related, via "grave," to the human proclivity to dig beneath the surface so as to build, at once, places for the dead in the earth, and foundations for buildings to be built above the earth, places for the living. The "grave," place of burial of the body and marked limit of the individual life, imitates and adds to the force of gravity upon all bodies, not only fixing them, as the bodies of individual lives, in one place, but allowing for the double process of perception and abstraction, experience and inscription that, together, form the basis not of history itself, the *facta* of bodies living and dead, but of reflection upon those facts and bodies, possible historical knowledge.

Apposite to continuous motion, a natural, Lucretian dance of shapes in space, and the artificial channeling of energy by technology, gravity is to the irreducibly material bodies borne by the earth as the referent is to the merely formal, and thus semantically transformable, bodies borne by language: a placement, or "where," allowing for the perception of an individual, historical body over time. As gravity neither possesses nor attaches to any single body, much less entity, itself, but allows for the posing of substance, so the referent allows for the proposal of meaning, creating, within the infinite movement of production of meaning, a *point de repère.* And because language, in all its lawless figurality and its self-defining grammatical laws, is a distinctly nonphysical, artificial, and human force, language must go beyond or beneath the superficial placement of life defined by natural laws: the physical equilibrium between the vertical force of gravity and the horizontal perspective of living bodies, whether in motion or at rest; and the balance of forces tending downward and outward, that yield surfaces of performance as well as trajectories of flight, a basis for action and movement as well as reflection and the impetus to thought.

Language must do more than move and position if it is to have additional, specifically referential force, a power exerted upon the mind that pulls it outside itself to something neither conceivable nor visible in itself, something the mind can neither think nor perceive of its own means alone. Burying beneath the surface so as to allow for building upon the surface, site of archeology as well as memory, imagination, and the mobility of linguistic forms, the referent simulates what we cannot see—the force of gravity—but attempts to do so within language itself. And so, in order to do so, it must exaggerate and extend gravity's effects, making the invisible visible by adding, with the necessary help of instruments or tools, human energy to natural force, situating by engraving—placing within by displacing—the matter of the earth.[5]

5. The "weighty" significance of the interplay of "grave," "engrave," and gravity is perhaps best demonstrated in Goethe's novel, albeit negatively, by the fungibility of meaning instead attributed to the glass etched with Eduard's initials, that, having been drained of drink and ritually tossed in the air by the mason at the close of the foundation/memorial stone-laying ceremony, is serendipitously caught by someone before it can fall and break (VI:302–3). It is this engraved glass spared from shattering, whose "E" and "O" he subsequently interprets as his and Ottilie's initials, that comes to stand in Eduard's mind for the rightness of his and Ottilie's love. And it was "in the place" of this glass, as he announces to the Hauptmann in Part Two, that Eduard had then decided to make his own body a "sign," one whose new, exclusive meaning would be the propriety of his relationship with Ottilie, if, upon going into battle, his body, like the glass, remained intact: "'So will I make myself,' I called to myself, as I spent so many doubtful hours in that lonely place, 'so will

In doing so it also renders visible its additional temporal effect. For, just as "grave," verb and noun, act and thing, is not only a spacing, but a *temporalization of space as place*—a making of place in the excising of matter and introduction, into matter, of space—so the artificial imitation of gravity, the construction, founded upon the burial, of the referent, produces, in its marked spatiality and marking exaggeration, the possibility, foreign to the apparent, physical world, of the conception and perception of time. Built "deep" into the earth, such a referent makes "gravity" "serious," adding, through artifice, the extra "weight" of the imperceptible, of time, to the force that holds us at any moment on earth.[6] Alternately visible and invisible,

---

I make myself into a sign, in the place of the glass, of whether our relationship is possible or not. I go and seek death, not as a madman, but as one who hopes to live. Ottilie is meant to be the prize I am fighting for'" (VI:447).

It is precisely the untethered circulation and opportunistic semantic employment of the letters inscribed on the fragile, mobile glass—used first, as denotative writing, to commemorate Eduard's existence; next, as ritual drinking vessel, in the ceremonial grounding of the *Lusthaus*; then, as symbolism, wondrously saved from destruction, for the enduring love between Eduard and Ottilie; and, finally, for the telos of Eduard's own mortal life, now modeled upon it, as a "sign"—that distinguish the act of engraving, as incised writing on any surface, fit for application to many purposes, from the especially "serious," placed and place-forming, art of engraving discussed here, that which constitutes not a visible and meaningfully adaptable sign but rather a "secret," "buried" referent, the "grave" and gravity of the earth-bound.

6. Similar to the purposeful exaggeration of word and action by the baroque, the artificially exaggerated application of force involved in investing language with gravity—burying the referent, placing stone in the earth, marking the spot—is perfectly represented in Goethe's succinct description of Charlotte's ceremonial wielding of a "hammer" in order to effect "the joining of the stone with the ground" in the laying of the *Lusthaus* "groundstone": "To Charlotte and the others the hammer was then given, so that, through a triple pounding, the joining of the stone with the ground could be *expressly* sealed" (VI:302 [emphasis added]). It is, of course, the same Charlotte, described here as "expressly" hammering the groundstone into place in a public ritual, who is described elsewhere as casually removing the stones marking the place of the dead from the churchyard. In ascribing to one of its characters the performance of these two opposing roles, Goethe's novel indicates that, whatever the temporary view one holds, and use one makes, of the demarcated matter

by turns physical and metaphysical, the architecture of the referent, of linguistic "gravity," may well be covered over, as Goethe's Mason remarks, with all the superficial structures and "ornamental figures" that accompany living, the passions and actions, lovemaking and landscaping, that engage the living at any time: that is its history as a particular physical thing. Yet, because the particularity of this thing is nothing other than its historicity, its physical reality is rendered metaphysical as soon as that historicity is conceived. The secret of its burial, and surprise of its later unearthing, gives the historical referent the "gravity" of uniquely temporal significance: the "seriousness" of the limits of historical experience, inscribed in abstraction from any individual experience, now made palpable not only individually but in principle in the presence of a marked, material form.

There need, of course, be no "referent," one can only suppose, just as buildings don't have to last—they can be posed, transposed, disposable. The dead, too, we know, don't have to be buried but can be made weightless, *antigrav*, as insubstantial as the idea of life as pure circulation, pure language, or divine myth, to which, out of desire, belief, or ideology, they can be conceptually joined, just as they can be made to disappear from the graveyard of history, to leave no trace anywhere, no " 'here' " (to recall Lanzmann's ghostly deictic of place). And writing—although this is harder to imagine in any society that writing has ruled—need never be affixed as sign, artificial emblem of gravity, to any part of the ground. It was, after all, in the course of redefining language, as a purely differential system of signs, that Saussure was compelled to redefine the "sign" as the

---

of which one takes hold, only the burial and removal of such matter from sight—from *aesthesis*, whether symbolic (as in the case of the changing meaning of Eduard's glass) or abstract (as in Charlotte's meaninglessly pleasing graveyard design)—may make its significance, as inscription in the ground, a "grave" or "serious" matter for those who do, and will, live upon it. Whether we build and commemorate, or aestheticize and destroy commemoration, it is the "joining of stone with the ground," the supplemental, artificial union making and marking a place, that, engraving the remains of experience—the naturally unfathomable history of relations—may remain the basis for others' unanticipated future experience, a referent.

union of "concept" and "acoustic image," precisely so as to distinguish it from the "current usage" equating sign with its "sensuous" or "material" aspect alone.[7] Just as Saussure's revolutionary notion of the sensory-conceptual sign ensured at once its freedom from reduction to the image of a sign—as mechanical label or signpost, on one end of the spectrum of images, or mystical embodiment of being, on the other—and its availability, from within the differential limits of each synchronic situation, to infinite conceptual metamorphosis and use, so need language never be related, in any nonlinguistic *or* nonmystical way, to the historical, to the actuality and pastness of events. In this aspect alone akin to pure technology and pure biology—energies channeled without intervention of consciousness and so perfectly free, in themselves, to feed upon themselves—language that, ever molting, lives by shedding its skins, can momentarily make but, of itself, never mark a context, never fix in time any one in the stream of signs, "the flow of discourse," it sloughs off.[8]

The gravity of language, however, lies elsewhere, and not within language alone. Language calls that earthly pull from itself "the referent," and so do we all, even as we only refer to it, but its force is made available to the individual mind when its place in space is encountered in time, and that place is never given, by language or the earth, but marked, unearthed, built.

7. Saussure, *Cours*, pp. 98–99.

8. The reference here is to Lessing's remarkable observation, in *Laokoon* XVI, that even when for Homer "it is only a matter of the image, he will disperse this image into a kind of history of the object . . . in order to let the parts of it keep pace with the flow of speech" (or "discourse" [*Fluss der Rede*]) (Lessing, *Sämtliche Schriften*, IX: 100.)]. It is precisely the dispersal of the "parts of the object" over "history"—the life of the object transmitted in its always partial historical afterlife—that a "flow of discourse" as such, one which would disentangle discourse from historical objects, and its own temporally enduring referents, denies. This is discourse as Mephisto—in his "own" unstoppable words, "*Der Geist, der stets verneint*" ("The spirit that continually negates [or denies]" [*Faust I,* 1338])—whereas literature is discourse as Faust, daring to join with discourse "to act" against discourse, to create a "new" ground *and* "the trace" of its "own" "earthly days," a "place" at which spirit will instead find itself, lingering.

APPENDIX

Continuation of Notes

PART I, N. 2

Considering "the fundamental concerns of the play to be epistemological and aesthetic" (26), rather than the illustration of one man's (failed) moral education, Brown indirectly suggests an inherent conflict between artificial forms of knowledge and Goethe's recognition of the unartful movement of time: "to enter time is to enter change . . . Nature and temporality are inseparable . . . To enter the world is to enter the temporal flux. While it may seem obvious that to live in the world and to live in time are identical, it was not obvious to Faust in 'Night,' when as a human subject to time he sought to transcend the world" (81). Such "transcend[ence]," however, can only be effected in a complete identification with "temporal flux," one that preempts the very experience of temporality, and, as Brown rightly points out, such identification must lead *in literary terms* not to the imitation of nature but rather to naturally ungrounded artificiality. As this study argues, and Brown, however, does not emphasize, it is precisely the architectural project of constructing a ground independent of nature and history that ends Faust's immersion in the temporal world. On the pointedly allegorical mode of the *Faust II*, cf. also Heinz Schlaffer, *Faust Zweiter Teil.*

Victor Lange interestingly interprets the openly "allegorical," "symbolic," and "citational character" of *Faust II* as "exceeding all figural and scenic representation" to compose a play whose real subject is its own staging of poetic acts: more than a drama, *Faust II*, Lange argues, is a dramatic poem, "a poem precisely about language, about the possibilities of communicative speech within an encompassing, realized system of rhetorical and poetological means of representation and expression" (Lange, "*Faust*" pp. 287, 293–94). See also the fine essay by Clark S. Muenzer, "Goethe's Goethic Classicism," in which the "abruptly changing stage" of the play, like the figure of Helena herself, "dragged across time and space as *Übertragung* into Faust's palace," are shown to enact Goethe's "essentially *historical aesthetic*" in Part Two (pp. 188, 200).

Although Muenzer does not treat the building project of Act V, his observation that "Goethe has layered the *Faust-* stage temporally" provides an especially fitting description of the very layers of temporal nonidentity—of theory and practice, conception and vision—that Faust would violently collapse in the construction of a "newest earth" "free," precisely, from all previous stagings of time. A consonant view of Helen's spectral identity in the play, and of all identities in a "state" of war, is offered in Jan Miekowski's excellent "Faust at War" (forthcoming).

Brown—whose interpretation of the play's many internal stagings as pointedly artificial, world-literary and allegorical, rather than mimetic or narrative in intention, Muenzer's "historical aesthetic" most resembles—returns to *Faust* in the context of opera in *The Persistence of Allegory*, pp. 214–15.

PART I, N. 13

Gernot Böhm, while clearly taking into account the destruction of the existent context that is part and parcel of Faust's building project—"The project of Faust is violent and ruthless with regard to that which exists, the elderly, represented by Philemon and Baucis. It is totalizing"—oddly interprets Goethe's indirect or reported descriptions of the bloody, unindividuated labor of Faust's "slaves," "called up" from "their camp" (V. 11503) as "a magical technological process," an "allegorical representation" (see Böhme, *Goethes Faust*, pp. 159–60). In a related comment on Goethe's rejection of Newton's forceful production of prismatic color from light in favor of a process of experimentation within the "realm of nature," "the immediate region of the living," Werner Heisenberg compares the modern theoretical physicist, who "leaves behind the realm of living perception," with an "alpinist" who must steadily climb higher "in order to oversee the land beneath him in its contexts": "the higher he climbs, the wider the land opens itself to his view, but the sparer also becomes the life that surrounds him," until "finally, he reaches a blindingly clear region . . . in which all life has died" (Heisenberg, "Die Goethesche und Newtonische Farbenlehre," p. 432). Claiming "we can be sure that to Goethe, the poet [rather than scientist], this last and purest clarity, toward which science strives, was fully known," Heisenberg ascends higher than Goethe writing as poet or as scientist—Goethe, who represents the desire for such an exhaustive visual perspective in *Faust* and *Die Wahlverwandtschaften*, *while* contradictorily including the "region of the living," of passion and temporality, within it.

Perhaps the clearest statement of Faust's rationale for the removal of the couple is offered by John Gearey (*Goethe's Other Faust*, p. 168):

> The removal of the old couple does not mean for Faust an extension of the land for the inhabitancy of a greater number for the greater good, it means

> the opportunity and pleasure of contemplating his achievement which alone completed the conscious goal of human action . . . This is the Faust who has sought absolute beauty and now seeks absolute completion, which are perhaps the same thing.

When, however, Gearey follows this lucid analysis of the aesthetic basis for murder with the remarkable judgment and summation of Faust, "*He remains the idealist*" (168, my emphasis), the brutality as well as the materiality of Faust's aestheticist building project vanish from view, much in the same manner, if from the opposite point of view, of those who praise Faust instead for his "communal" striving. Along with Lukács and Berman, these include Blackhall, who, in his enthusiasm for Faust's attempt to build a ground for a transcendentally "free people" neglects to mention Philemon and Baucis altogether:

> The ground is free, the people are free—or rather: the ground is to be free, the people are to be free, for Faust makes it clear that what he is describing is not something that exists but something that he wishes shall exist . . . new earth . . . full of potentialities for development, uncluttered because new and therefore free for men to develop. Free people means people free to develop the potentialities of the free ground, free to work together in this common undertaking (Blackhall, *Faust's Last Speech*, pp. 6–7).

An excellent account of Lukács's "dogmatic interpretation of *Faust*," in which the paradigmatic status of "the Philemon/Baucis episode as the brutal attack of capitalism on the pre-capitalist idyll" is itself viewed as necessary by the "Marxist-Stalinist vista of human development" espoused by Lukács, then writing in Moscow—the aesthetic embrace of the clearing of any individual obstacles to what Lukács called "the unstoppable progress of the human species" as a "totality"—is offered by Nicholas Vazsonyi in *Lukács Reads Goethe*, pp. 119–26. A noteworthy exception to the common critical idealization of Faust is offered by Gerhard Kaiser in *Ist der Mensch zu Retten?* Kaiser recognizes and underscores both the totalizing, antihistorical impulse of Faust's "idyllic" building project and the profoundly "unsocial" absolutism required for its realization, but without taking into consideration the necessary condition of the latter, Faust's desire to "collapse" theory "into" praxis and place into origin: "The newest earth is determined by Faust to be an idyll in toto. Idyll and dynamic society are supposed to collapse into one. The totalized idyll is everything in everything, and it is a posthistorical state like escatological fulfillment . . . For the sake of an imaginary free humanity [Faust] reduces human beings here and now into human material" (60–61).

PART I, N. 16

Heidegger's original German reads:

> Was ist die moderne Technik? Auch sie ist ein Entbergen . . .
>
> Das in der modernen Technik waltende Entbergen ist ein Herausfordern, das an die Natur das Ansinnen stellt, Energie zu liefern, die als solche herausgefördert und gespeichert werden kann. Gilt dies aber nicht auch von der alten Windmühle? Nein. Ihre Flügel drehen sich zwar im Winde, seinem Wehen bleiben sie unmittelbar anheimgegeben. Die Windmühle erschliesst aber nicht Energien der Luftströmung, um sie zu speichern. . . .
>
> Das Wasserkraftwerk ist in den Rheinstrom gestellt. Es stellt ihn auf seinen Wasserdruck, der die Turbinen daraufhin stellt, sich zu drehen, welche Drehung diejenige Maschine umtreibt, deren Getriebe den elektrischen Strom herstellt, für den die Überlandzentrale und ihr Stromnetz zur Strombeförderung bestellt sind. Im Bereich dieser ineinandergreifenden Folgen der Bestellung elektrischer Energie erscheint auch der Rheinstrom als etwas Betselltes. Das Wasserkraftwerk ist nicht in den Rheinstrom gebaut wie die alte Holzbrücke, die seit Jahrhunderten Ufer mit Ufer verbindet. Vielmehr ist der Strom in das Kraftwerk verbaut. Er ist, was er jetzt als Strom ist, nämlich Wasserdrucklieferant, aus dem Wesen des Kraftwerks. . . .
>
> Das Entbergen, das die moderne Technik durchherrscht, hat den Charakter des Stellens im Sinne der Herausforderung. Diese geschieht dadurch, dass die in der Natur verborgene Energie aufgeschlossen, das Erchlossene umgeformt, das Umgeformte gespeichert, das Gespeicherte wieder verteilt und das Verteilte erneut umgeschaltet wird. Erschliessen, umformen, speichern, verteilen, umschalten sind Weisen des Entbergens. . . .
>
> Wer vollzieht das herausfordernde Stellen, wodurch das, was man das Wirkliche nennt, als Bestand entborgen wird? Offenbar der Mensch. Inwiefern vermag er solches Entbergen? Der Mensch kann zwar dieses oder jenes so oder so vorstellen, gestalten und betreiben. Allein, über die Unverborgenheit, worin sich jeweils das Wirkliche zeigt oder entzieht, vefügt der Mensch nicht.

PART I, N. 20

The mutually entangled development of the terms that Riera expertly describes is directly relevant to the nonhistorical view of the split within *poiesis*, manifested instead in the possibility or impossibility of residing, that is offered in the present study, and, for reasons of its own revealing complexity, well worth quoting at length:

> "The Origin of the Work of Art" (1935–36) is inextricably implicated in "The Question Concerning Technology," in the same way that the latter is implicated in "The Origin of the Work of Art," as the 1956 Addendum

> bears witness. There are good reasons for this, since there is an *inextricable* relation between *poiesis* and *techne* that took Heidegger several years to explicate . . . There is an archi-original split of *Stellen* between *poiesis* and *techne* that opens up the two paths of unconcealment. The ambiguity of the essence of *techne* points to the secret of unveiling, of truth. *Poiesis* preserves the archi-originary, the *polemos*, the strife that *phusis* is . . . It is more originary than *techne*, since the latter forgets all about it. The essence of technology represses or hides this other mode of unveiling. (49)

Riera astutely notes that the close proximity in significance of *techne* and *poiesis* makes such a staggered delineation of their origination hardly tenable, and that it is "dwelling" that encompasses both terms under the aegis of *poiesis*, once *techne*, described previously as less "originary" than *poiesis*, is instead understood "in its origin" as *poiesis*: "Once again we come across the question of dwelling, since in its origin *techne* meant the unveiling that produces the truth of being in the radiance of what comes into presence, that is *poiesis*" (50). The difficulty in understanding *techne* as both originally *poiesis* and less originary than *poiesis*—the difficulty that the contrast between the power-plant, in the essay on technology, and the Greek temple, in the essay on the origin of art, makes all too plain—is ultimately described by Riera as constitutive of Heidegger's "turn toward the work of art and the poem," a turn whose own historical moment seems no less ambiguous than the "origin" of *techne*, since arising, in Riera's account, "in this context, punctuated by nihilism and the danger that the essence of technology harbors," which is to say, *after* the turn toward the work of art and the poem in the essay on the origin of art. The ambiguity of *poiesis* as *techne*, of its "two paths," as Riera states, remains as resistant to historicization—even that of a "step back" from conceptual history, in the Heideggerian sense—as to Heidegger's own untenable conflation of them under the auspices of dwelling.

PART II, N. 2

I have analyzed Goethe's novel and contemporaneous color theory as equally fundamental representations of the formation and experience of figural relations in "The Coloring of Relations"; see also Chapter 2 in *The Imposition of Form*, pp. 87–138. The interpretive studies devoted to Goethe's novel that have appeared over the past twenty years may well outnumber those of the preceding one hundred and eighty. Set in motion by the influx of theoretical textual approaches into *Germanistik*, and decline in significance of *Sittenkritik*, a variety of critical theses and principles have come to circle about the enigmatic *Wahlverwandtschaften* like so many planets orbiting a sun (or, in the novel's terms, much as "major" and "minor" characters turn about Ottilie). The present study attempts to chart the individual and intersecting paths of thought that continue to describe this ever-expanding universe, acknowledging them as part and parcel of the reflection upon ongoing historicity represented, under cover of its story of figural relations, in the text, while focusing less on any specific theoretical interpretation of the novel than the interrelated formative activities the novel represents as intrinsic to itself. For thorough historical overviews of the reception of the novel to date, see Astrid Orle Tantillo's invaluably detailed *Goethe's Elective Affinities and the Critics* and John Winkelmann's summation of the basic tendencies of the criticism in *Goethe's Elective Affinities*, pp. 1–33.

In addition to its theoretical conceptualization, recent years have seen an increased interest in relating *Die Wahlverwandtschaften* to Goethe's natural science writing, with markedly different results. In *Erzählen als Naturverhältnis*, Elisabeth von Thadden interprets the novel as an extension of one of the principle theoretical views underlying Goethe's natural science writing, as expressed in *Die Farbenlehre* and the key early essay, "Der Versuch als Vermittler zwischen Subjekt und Objekt" (1791), that a purely empirical study of nature is illusory in that natural phenomena are themselves "'first visible as Text'" (Preface to the *Farbenlehre*) (15). Thadden takes Goethe's well-known observation, in his advertisement for the novel (*Morgenblatt für gebildete Stände*, September 4, 1809), that the "'chemical figure of speech'" at the "'intellectual origin'" of the term "Wahlverwandtschaften" merely follows from the fact that "there is only *one* nature everywhere," as evidence that "science and literature in Goethe's works . . . are to be understood as correlated procedures for joining 'mimesis' with 'poiesis'" (14, 17). Thadden's emphasis upon the union of *mimesis* and *poiesis* effectively substitutes mimesis for its near opposite, the always transformative activity of experimentation in Goethe's science writings; analogously, as discussed shortly, it omits or discounts the significance of the architectural activity that, neither poetic nor mimetic, first takes apart, and then takes the place of "'nature'" "'everywhere'" in the novel. Cf. Susanne Konrad, in *Goethes "Wahlverwandtschaften,"* pp. 322–23, on the *Farbenlehre* as offering Goethe "intellectual access to reflection" through the dynamic of natural life. On the growing gap, by contrast, between Goethe's discursively and reflectively mediated natural science and the tendency of modern science toward increasing mathematical formalization, see John Neubauer, "'Die Abstraktion, vor der wir uns fürchten.'"

Interestingly, it was Solger, in an early letter to Abeken, who, while stating his own inability to express "the chain of thoughts" that the recently published *Wahlverwandtschaften* had provoked in him, goes on to attribute such expressive power to the *Farbenlehre*: "The *Color Theory* also surprised me to a certain extent. God knows I had formed no particular expectation of it in advance; I believed that at most I would find in it mere experiments. Well, here is a book in which nature has become alive, human, and colloquial. It seems to me it also sheds some light on the *Wahlverwandtschaften*," (Karl Wilhelm Friedrich Ferdinand Solger to Bernhard Rudolf Abeken, 18 October 1810 in Härtl, ed., *Eine Dokumentation*, p. 172).

PART II, N. 3

While Fries somewhat loosely equates metaphor with image, later describing the term "Wahlverwandtschaften" as "*ein Bild für das Bild*" (131) [an image for the image], the novel distinguishes "Gleichnisrede" [figure of speech]—used by Eduard and the Hauptmann to discuss "Wahlverwandtschaften" in relation to the natural world (Part One, Chap. IV [VI:270])—from "*Bild*," used throughout the novel to indicate either a painted or living likeness, as well as their combination in *tableaux vivants*. John Noyes astutely interprets all "choice" in the novel as "blind," because based on a persuasion of "visible" "meaning" that conceals the necessarily historical nature of the "sign": "the becoming-visible of the world" entails the "unreliability of the visible sign . . . For behind the visibility of life lies the delimiting, the difference of death that allow unity," "the trace of the not-happened in the happened" that constitutes "the problem of the sign," in which "meaning and visibility are fundamentally different" (Noyes, "Die blinde Wahl," p. 133.

At the opposite end of the interpretive spectrum from Fries and Noyes, Jeremy Adler initially describes "*Wahlverwandtschaften*" as the "idea" of Goethe's novel, and an "idea" as being for Goethe both an "abstract, philosophical concept" and a "plan," but proceeds—by way of lists enumerating specific, supposedly "analogical" quantities (chemical elements and processes on the one hand and fictional characters and emotional processes on the other), and charts and diagrams symbolizing fictional and chemical events deemed similarly comparable—to apply, with a literalism as breathtaking as it is burdensome, the details of the chemical theories of Goethe's day to his novel. See Adler, *"Eine fast magische Anziehungskraft"*, p. 18; and especially Chapter One, "Die Idee der *Wahlverwandtschaften*" (17–31) and Chapter Four, "Die 'Wahlverwandtschaften' in Goethes Roman" (140–216). In direct contrast to Adler, Robert David Gould (*Elective Affinities*) and, more recently, Peter D. Smith (*Metaphor and Materiality*), understand Goethe's use of the term, "*Wahlverwandtschaften*," along more general, theoretical lines, Gould emphasizing that Goethe's scientific and literary writing strive equally to represent "the basic principles according to which the processes of life operate" (Gould, p. 280), and Smith reminding us that, at once empirically oriented, or "guided by the phenomenon," and attentive to the human mediation of all observation, Goethe's scientific writing maintained "the interrelation of humankind and nature" (Smith, pp. 79, 57).

Smith's emphasis on Goethe's guiding conception of one encompassing nature always in process of "becoming" is shared by Monika Hielscher (*Natur and Freiheit in Goethes "Die Wahlverwandtschaften,"* p. 86), who argues, however, that Goethe's "*one* nature" includes within it the possibility of "'free'" human decisions (137). Ann-Theres Faets (*"Überall unreine Natur"?*), by contrast, interprets Goethe's "reference to a chemical model" and "announcement of a unifying power of nature" as merely intended "polemically," arguing that "art first arises through form" and nature offers the artist "no ordering function" (26, 61). Faets ably disputes Adler's characterization of the novel as directly derivative of contemporary theoretical chemistry (198–99n79), but, in asserting Goethe's "emancipation of art production from the process of the imitation of nature" (44), she indicates an understanding of nature rather unlike Goethe's, for whom nature and form were precisely not opposed but rather integrated life principles: the common thrust of Goethe's voluminous natural science writings is that natural phenomena, not unlike the things of human nature, are products of a constant process of transformation. While Faets is certainly right to point out that imitation of nature is never at issue in the novel, the arts of imitation—expressions of the distinctly human capacity and proclivity for mimetic imaging—are everywhere in this story, and the objects of such imitative images in the novel are always peculiarly human as well. Like Faets, Harriet Murphy (*The Rhetoric of the Spoken Word*) rejects Adler's view of the novel as an illustration of then current chemical paradigms, stating that readers who, attracted by the novel's descriptions of "chemical affinity or attraction," attribute these to "the realm of the personal world of human relationship [. . .] have been successfully misled" (72–73), thereby confirming but also re-enacting, one might add, the conceptual misdirection of the characters themselves. Arguing that *Die Wahlverwandtschaften* presents a "modern" enactment of a failed utopia, Johannes Twardella ("Experimente im Treibhaus der Moderne") similarly opposes the notion of "one nature" represented in Goethe's use of the chemical term, overlooking the figural basis and content of the term itself when he observes that relations "between people," unlike those in nature, "do not proceed mechanically" (448).

Finally, writing in the *Goethe-Jahrbuch* in 1906, Oskar Walzel early concluded that Goethe's use in the novel of a figure of speech taken from the natural sciences was "self-evident" (see Walzel, "Goethes 'Wahlverwandtschaften'"). Commenting on Goethe's observation to Riemer (24 July 1809) that "moral symbols in natural sciences" are "more meaningfully [*geistreicher*] and aptly combined with poetry and society," Walzel cuts through the Gordian knot of the irresolvably ambiguous basis of the figure to begin with, stating: "This is self-evident; for in [poetry and society] it is only a matter of repositioning the morality that has been applied to nature back into the intellectual realm" (54).

PART II, N. 5

By contrast, recent criticism, when it has considered the pervasive presence of architectural activity in the novel at all, has most often viewed it retrospectively as an historically limited phenomenon, the symptom of a weakened, moribund, or, alternatively, self-regenerating propertied class. Criticism in this vein includes Norbert W. Bolz's conflation of architecture with the "image" or images it houses, specifically those of the "too narrow" and thus failed "bourgeois" attempt to "construct the completely unconstructable—*Dasein*" in the novel (see Bolz, "Ästhetisches Opfer," esp. pp. 77–80); Werner Schlick's extensive discussion and subsequent dismissal of all architectural activity in the novel as dilettantism characteristic of a decadent social order, despite his reliance, via Hans R. Vaget (see esp. "'Ein reicher Baron,'" pp. 123–61), on the essay on dilettantism in which Goethe defined the latter as lacking specifically in "architectonic" "power" (see Schlick, *Goethe's Die Wahlverwandtschaften*, esp. Chapter II: "Goethe's Aesthetic Principles and their Application to Artistic Training in *Die Wahlverwandtschaften*," pp. 39–70, and Chapter III: "The Characters' Practices in the Park Project," pp. 71–164); and Stephen Blessin's opposite interpretation of the characters' preoccupation with building as their attempt, in the aftermath of the French Revolution, to "renew" a social order rendered vulnerable (Blessin, *Die Romane Goethes*, esp. pp. 89–101; this interpretation is repeated in Blessin, *Goethes Romane* p. 235). Blessin's earlier analysis of the novel, from the perspective of communications theory, states rather more interestingly that what he calls "the things in the novel, the moss hut, the paths, the lake, etc., have no meaning in themselves," before subordinating these "things" to an undefined "sense" given them by the characters (see Blessin, *Erzählstruktur und Leserhandlung*, p. 48). Blessin's astute appraisal, in that early study, of the new and enduring difficulties this particular novel presents "to the reader's understanding" (p. 10), includes a persuasive critique of reception theory, as at once too concrete, or dependent, in H. R. Jauss's own terms, on "the facticity of the transmitted," and too abstract, or ready to equate "literary work and historical facticity" within a general "whole" of "historical totality" (p. 179; pp. 177–80).

Contrary to Blessin, A. G. Steer, Jr. (in *Goethe's Elective Affinities*), while reproducing Friedrich Nemec's attempt at an actual "sketch" of Eduard's and Charlotte's estate (160) (see Nemec, *Die Ökonomie*), views architectural activity in the novel as a sign not of the characters' wish for revitalization but rather of their "infect[ion] with the virus of boredom and inactivity," of having "nothing else, really, to do" (21). Steer extends his description of characters building out of boredom to Goethe's own "boring descriptions" of building in the novel before attributing both to a supposed "indictment" by Goethe "of many of the contemporary land-holding nobility," "the decaying feudal aristocracy of his age" whom Goethe, according to Steer, envelops in his narrative as if in a poisoned "robe of Nessus" (21, 163, 170, 298). Like Nemec and Steer, Hans M. Wolff offers a concrete model of the novel's built landscape, but for Wolff that model is the actual estate, outside Jena, of the family of Silvie von Ziegesar; according to Wolff, it is not social criticism but secret love that motivates Goethe's detailed account of building by the landed gentry. (Wolff, *Goethe in der Periode der Wahlverwandtschaften*). Acknowledging Goethe's attachment to von Ziegesar and visits to her family's estate, while arguing for the insignificance of such biographical detail to the novel, Hans Reiss views *Die Wahlverwandtschaften* as a "drama . . . of the four main characters" and interprets its architectural components ("the hut," "the house," "the arbour," "the lake" and "lay-out of the park") as subordinate "images" and "symbols" of the characters' inner lives and dramatic development (see Reiss, *Goethe's Novels*, pp. 145, 161–66).

In "View from the Summerhouse: Goethe's *Wahlverwandtschaften* and its Literary Successors" (pp. 145–60), Judith Ryan recognizes the structural importance of architectural activity to the novel, describing "the move from the moss hut to the summer house" as "the central axis of the novel's development" (p. 145), before equating that activity with a process of "Verinnerlichung" [internalization] by which both moss hut and summer house become "symbols of the unreality and insubstantiality of late 19th century social life" (p. 160), while Theo Elm, by contrast, views the same development, from a "moss hut á la Rousseau" to "a decadent 'pleasure-building,'" as indicative of the historical "dialectic of progress and obsolescence" that produces cognitive change (see Elm, "'Wissen' und 'Verstehen' in Goethes *Wahlverwandtschaften*," pp. 91–92), and Smith, by still further contrast, identifies the architectural interventions in nature in the novel not with a critique of contemporary German society but with Goethe's all-encompassing, non-historicist view of life on earth, finding in Charlotte's attention to "context", as it is raised in her discussions of landscape gardening, "the motif" that "is central to the narrative and reflects Goethe's concept of the ultimate unity of the natural world" (see Smith, *Metaphor and Materiality*, p. 56).

Unlike Smith, Thadden draws a negative contrast between the acts of building represented in the fiction and what Goethe figuratively called the "materials for the building" of his natural science theory. Limiting her consideration of architectural activity in the novel to the foundation-laying and construction of the "Lusthaus" and the "rule-oriented architecture," in "the French-style," she claims characterizes the "antiquarian" landscaping plans of the gardener, she criticizes the former as "rushed" and the latter as "behind the times in that it aims to "domesticat[e] nature into an architectonic object"

(Thadden, *Erzählen als Naturverhältnis*, pp. 218–20; for a similar view of non-homogeneous temporality in general in the novel, see Joseph Vogl, "Nomos der Ökonomie," esp. 508: "Time here means hesitation and acceleration, action itself, again and again, loss of time or hurry, delay or haste"). Rather than considering Goethe's use of the term "building" [*Gebäude*] to describe the shaping of his own natural science writings, and the pervasive representation of acts of building by his novel, as significant, Thadden criticizes the characters' drive to build as detracting from the mimesis of their story as natural history, poor competition for what she, contrary to Goethe, calls the "living architect, nature" (210). Still, her unusual characterization of non-natural architectural activity in the novel as temporally out of step—either overly hasty or outmoded, too fast or too slow—hints revealingly at a disturbance of the sequential experience of time by the architectural. Disputing the "concept of myth" that dominates modern interpretations of the novel, and "whose most prominent representative . . . is Walter Benjamin," Faets helpfully notes that the characters are driven neither by mythic forces nor "fate," whether "natural" or supernatural, but, rather, on the contrary, by the impulse to transform nature "architectonically" and "imagistically": "the characters of the novel alter the nature which surrounds them . . . proceeding to do so architectonically and in a painterly-imagistic way" (Faets, *"Überall nur eine Natur?"* pp. 12–13).

Among the early readers of the novel who remarked readily upon its extensive involvement of architecture in the life of its characters, Wilhelm von Humboldt, while ultimately commending the work, complains first of the "dryness" and "superfluity" of its detailed relation of the characters' "external life, the park grounds, and so forth" (Humboldt to Friedrich Gottlieb Welcker, 23 Dec. 1809, in Härtl, ed., *Eine Dokumentation*, p. 88). A few decades later, Grillparzer objected astutely to the "near parallel" "importance" accorded architectural matters and plot development in the novel, cannily criticizing the former as merely "ways to pass (or more literally, to banish [*Zeitvertrieb*]) time":

> What is most bothersome in this *Wahlverwandtschaften* is the obnoxious importance which, from the very beginning, is given to the park grounds, the most minute (or insignificant) built things, and similar stuff, an importance that nearly parallels that of the main action. It is as if one were reading a piece out of Goethe's life, in which he had partially paralyzed his incomparable talents so as to participate almost as much in mere ways of passing time as in the most important occasions of the calling that is most his own. There should, however, be a hierarchy of interest, and that which one wastes on secondary things will always be taken from the main thing. (Franz Grillparzer, diary entry of 1841, rpt. in Ursula Ritzenhoff, ed., *Erläuterungen und Dokumente*, p. 166.)

The third published review of the novel (*Jenaische Allgemeine Literatur-Zeitung*, Nr. 16 and 17, 18–19 Jan. 1810), by Johann Delbrück (who had earlier reviewed *Die natürliche Tochter* at Goethe's request), realized Grillparzer's apprehension of the near "parallel" "importance" accorded architecture and action in the novel, but without judging that parallelism problematic. Delbrück begins his review with a precise linear summary of the different architectural activities engaged in by the individual characters as "they so eagerly strive to order and to shape all that which in the world is given over to their dominion." Only subsequently and separately does he summarize its other story, the development of the characters' passions. (See Härtl, ed. *Eine Dokumentation*, pp. 114–21). It is fair to say that, up to, since, and including Benjamin's essay on the novel (pub. 1924–25), and despite the contextualization of "the image" within the architectural that will characterize Benjamin's later writings, no subsequent review or interpretation of the novel has questioned the interrelation of building and image, or the central presence of building itself, in the novel.

PART II, N. 8

In Goethe, by contrast, the context defined by the architectural is less constitutive, in metonymic fashion, of an entire playing field of fleeting, always acquirable objects of desire, than of the delimited, artificial place in which motive passion, shaped instead into specific relation, into figuration, not only arises but endures, memorialized in story, image, and, ultimately (in Ottilie's painted vault), in the merging of these with the architectural itself.

Dickson also compares the foregrounded narrative function of the architectural in Balzacian realism and the topographical in Goethe's novel, suggesting that, whereas in Balzac the prominence of "concentrated scenic elements," such as "Mme Vauquer's boarding-house," appears attributable to the authorial "autonomy" of the narrator, in *Die Wahlverwandtschaften* "the whole of [the] landscape is described piecemeal and only in the closest association with character and events" (see Dickinson, "Spatial Concentration and Themes," p. 162; on the joint material and conceptual importance of the "piecemeal" to the novel's description of nature, see section three below, "Nature in Pieces"). Proceeding to distinguish Goethe's implementation of landscape from its predominantly symbolic use in early twentieth-century fiction, Dickson makes the point that, rather than serving as "an esoteric device" or "set of recondite mathematical symbols" in the manner of the "later European novel" of "Joyce and Mann," the "deictic function" of the "realistic landscape" Goethe has "constructed" in *Die Wahlverwandtschaften* always points to the story itself, its "concentrated *mise-en-scène*" "only affect[ing] the reader . . . as it affects one or more characters" (173). One can see in Dickson's opposition of the topographical to the symbolic Benjamin's analogous and complementary insight into the close relationship of the architectural and allegorical (discussed in section two). The architectural contextualization of "realist" representation by Goethe and Balzac that Dickson importantly notes does not lend itself, however, to strictly chronological delimitation. The allegorical tradition in realist fiction he helpfully describes continues into the twentieth century, in differing degrees, in works by Proust, Kafka, Rilke, Woolf, Dos Passos, and Broch, among others, and returns with renewed force throughout the writings of Sebald.

PART II, N. 10

Both Gabriele Brandstetter, in "Gesten des Verfehlens," and Waltraud Wiethölter, in "Von der Anstalt des Wissens," note that visual "images" are first named as such in the novel when seen from the apertures of the moss hut; they ascribe the "framed," "excerpted" nature of these views to the "encyclopedic" impulse of Goethe's time rather than the architectural impulse in Goethe's novel. In "'From hence they resolve all Beings to Eyes'" Tim Mehigan discusses the novel in the context of "Blickfetischismus" [fetishism of looking] in the enlightenment, a fixation on optical knowledge he identifies equally with the perceptual limitations set by Kant's critical philosophy and their near antithesis, the equation of the ocular and the infinite by such idealists as Berkeley; in the images framed by the apertures of the moss hut in particular Mehigan sees "the view of nature that seventeenth-century moral philosophy also strived to reveal" (174, 176). In "'Kunstgriffe' oder Poiesis der Mortifikation," Claudia Öhlschläger acknowledges that the "unfolding of the rhetorical effectivity of the chemical figure of speech"—i.e., the story of *Wahlverwandtschaften*—takes place in "the framed scenery" provided by "the castle and its garden lay-out," further noting that the "framing" of views into "images," occurring first in the moss hut, instills in Eduard the sense of an "imaginary 'added value'" resulting in his desire to "to add more people" to the novel's "action," and thereby ultimately "explod[ing]" the frame that ignited his imagination in the first place (188). While dynamic progressions like these beyond the confines of the image do indeed occur across the wide spectrum of imaging represented in the novel—the portraits of Ottilie in the side-chapel, the living imitation of acts of imaging, or *tableaux vivants*, the manic mimicry and beloved monkey of Luciane, "the tale of the wonderful neighboring children" that turns out to represent people present, as well as the cryptic reflections on "the image" presented as cited "from Ottilie's diary" (discussed further in section two)—and while these transgressions of the borders of the image, among others, may all accurately be seen in turn as a series of illustrations of the natural history of figuration, it should also be noted that none of the mises en scène of the image narrated in the novel take place in a "natural" or un-architected context. In contrast to Öhlschlager, Elisabeth Hermann views the prominent implementation of images in the novel as attempts to "fix . . . and petrify life" and so "suppress" the reality of death (Hermann, *Die Todesproblematik*, pp. 99–141 [99]).

The way in which the novel nearly merges synchronic with diachronic forms of representation, thereby vitiating their critical cognitive difference, is suggested by Blessin's excellent account of the interaction in the novel of story and image. Without noting the emphasis placed throughout the narrative on the *architecturally* established contiguity of its participants, Blessin notes: "Image and story . . . do not stand behind or next to each other in *Die Wahlverwandtschaften*. They are rather intimately interwoven" (*Goethes Romane*, 225). Observing generally that, "in the image time stands still" (228), Blessin nonetheless recognizes at least one instance in the novel in which images are viewed as inadequate to the task of arresting time, Eduard's discovery that, once Ottilie is dead, her movements on earth materially rather than merely apparently arrested, the beautiful "image of Ottilie in heaven" cannot suffice to recall her "living person"—a mimetic failing for which Eduard compensates by resorting again to contiguity, installing Ottilie's corpse in a side-chapel "residence" "*among the living*"(225, 221 [emphasis added]). By attributing Eduard's insistence on housing the dead Ottilie, rather than merely viewing images of her living, to the trademark "obstinacy" of his character's personality, Blessin, however, overlooks the larger pattern in the novel by which the "life" of images and human relations alike is made contingent upon their grounding, placement, and containment in architecture.

In *Einfall der Bilder*, Heike E. Brandstädter investigates the "inarticulate" aspect of all language that inheres in its inclusion of the imaged, or the figural, commending Goethe's novel for its heightened representation of this tension within language itself: "The particularity of the *Wahlverwandtschaften* . . . lies in the constitutive manner of its connection of language with figurality" [*Bildlichkeit*] (5). For Brandstädter, this connection is best represented in Ottilie—"that figure who is almost exclusively represented in images" (6). Its emphasis upon the insistent imaging in the novel of that character whose only observable character trait, one might add, seems to be the very ability to induce her own imaging, and concomitant neglect of the equally pervasive artifice of architecture in the novel, indicate the deeper ambiguity or tension inhabiting Brandstädter's fine study of "the image": the confusion—ironically, perhaps, linguistically induced—of rhetorical with physical and pictoral images (all referred to by Brandstädter as *Bilder*), or of the linguistic and the aesthetic. Emphasizing her visibility without describing her appearance, the language used in the novel to refer to Ottilie is not figural, in the rhetorical sense, but, rather, so aestheticizing as to be nearly non-linguistic. Simply identified with "beauty" upon first arriving at the estate ("Beauty is a welcome guest everywhere" (VI:281), Ottilie's sensory presence is subsequently equated with the very condition of *aesthesis*, or sense perception—"light"—when appearing as a sacred image in a silent *tableau vivant* ("The whole image was all light" [Goethe, VI:405]). As developed in section two, it is indeed this insistent indication by the language of the novel of something or someone purely sensory, aesthetic, and inarticulate at its center, even as that language presents the story of the novel with apparent discursive realism, that so disturbed Benjamin in the novel's representation of Ottilie, whose silent significance to the work as a whole brought the novel, for Benjamin, to the very brink of verbal nonsignification.

PART II, N. 15

Although Part II does suggest that the novel contains its own anti-mythical "antithesis" in the "Novelle" (pp. 103–7), the dominance of the extra-textual, anti-conceptual categories of fate and myth in the essay is maintained along a chain of related terms rapidly substituted for them until its end, inscrutable fate giving way to "*Neigung*" (p. 121) ["inclination"] (as opposed to "*die wahre Liebe*" (p. 122) ["true love"], "Rührung" (p. 127–28) ["that which moves ones"], "Hoffnung" (pp. 134–35) ("hope"), and finally "Schönheit" (pp. 128–30) ["beauty"], including the radical aesthetic hypostatization: "Schönes Leben, Wesentlich-Schönes and scheinhafte Schönheit, diese drei sind identisch" (p. 128) ["Beautiful life, (the) essentially beautiful and apparent beauty, these three are identical"]. The ultimate emphasis of the essay on a "beauty" that levels essence with appearance and appearance with life leads away from literary criticism and, fittingly, to a brief, remarkable discussion of the proper role of art criticism, that of acknowledging rather than critiquing the externality of the aesthetic itself: "Art criticism is not supposed to lift the outward shell but rather raise itself to the true perception of the beautiful through the most exacting recognition of the shell as shell" (p. 130). In this essay, in which nearly no trace of the novel's pervasive emphasis on specifically anti-mythical *and* anti-natural architectonic form is noted, Benjamin comes closest to "recognizing the outward shell as shell" in his extraordinary commentary and warning regarding Goethe's presentation of Ottilie, discussed shortly.

Cf. Rebecca Comay's excellent related observation, in "Materialist Mutations of the *Bilderverbot*" (pp. 337–78), that Benjamin's pervasive critique of myth included the form of myth itself, whose material externality contradicts its claim to "immanence": "Resurrection, as we read in the essay on Leskov, is in this sense to be conceived less as an idealizing transfiguration than as a radical disenchantment (*Entzauberung*): humanity's liberation from the 'nightmare' of mythic immanence . . . Such a demystification does not and cannot assume a (mythic) opposition between myth and enlightenment. The operative distinction would seem to work rather within the interstices of myth itself, at the point where myth overturns itself and point toward its own exterior" (357). Writing on the cusp of Benjamin's growing public reception, Barnes had already remarked critically of his interpretation of Goethe's novel: "Benjamin detects everywhere in the novel traces of Goethe's obsession with the mythical . . . sometimes com[ing] near to the method which he, not always justly, castigates in Friedrich Gundolf as 'mystification'" (Barnes, *Goethe's Novels*, p. 21).

PART II, N. 62

Arguing that the tension of the human pairings in Part One endows it with the aesthetic identity of Wölfflin's linearly closed form, while the lack of such "symmetrical" encounters in Part Two brings to mind the indeterminate, "painterly" aspect of Wölfflin's atectonic, Aulhorn describes the internal history of the novel as dispositive of the phases of Wölfflin's aesthetic history (109–110n). While Aulhorn's focus on interpersonal relations excludes from consideration the profoundly opposed acts of building performed by Charlotte and the mason, it is to these that Wöllflin's analysis perhaps most directly pertains. The nonsignifying painting-effect achieved by Charlotte's transformation of the graveyard from a place of formal determination into a pure space of undelineated coloration—a ground no longer of things fixed in the ground but, to use Aulhorn's general description of Part Two, of "something flowing" (110)—and the contrary burial of the groundstone as building foundation and containing memorial stone by the mason (discussed in the following section) read like realist, narrative allegories of Wölfflin's arthistorical *Grundbegriffe*.

If only for the sake of preserving the integrity and analytic value of those "fundamental concepts," it should be noted, however, that the kinds of aesthetic activity they indicate do not occur in the novel in the historical sequence Wölfflin indicates. While the burial of a groundstone that is also a tectonic, closed form containing bits of historical experience does indeed occur in Part One, that event is *accompanied* by the mason's discursive reflection upon the relation between its proper formal enactment and future meaning, a speech reported by the narrator as having already been translated of necessity out of its original "rhymed" form into "prose" (VI:299; discussed further in section 5 of this analysis, "Stones for Thought"). Similarly, it is the retrospective description of Charlotte's gravestone clearing ("we remember that . . .") and relation of the controversy ensuing from it that dominate the first chapter of Part Two (VI:361), while the act of *de*-signing the graveyard—of constructing or "ordering" *in its place* the "appearance of a pleasing space upon which the eye and imagination would gladly linger" (VI:254)—is narrated as having *already* occurred by the second chapter of Part One. Thus, while the application of the "Wölfflinian categories" of the tectonic and atectonic (Aulhorn, p. 109n) to the representation in the novel of the very activities they were originally conceived to describe—the making of closed, architectural form and painterly, or open design—does, in fact, tell us something significant about the relation of these forms and history, that relation, just as significantly, does *not* mirror the joining and separation of interpersonal relations that form the story of the novel's characters. This is not to say that the relation between signifying and nonsignifying aesthetic forms is not historical, i.e., at once historically marked and marking as every historical understanding of the aesthetic since Hegel's suggests, but rather that such a history of aesthetic forms does not resemble the metamorphoses of human relations—indeed, that it is only on the basis of the differentiating rather than mimetic relation between finished, material forms and the "something flowing" of human passions that the historical itself may be perceived, as the present study attempts to suggest).

BIBLIOGRAPHY

Primary Texts

Benjamin, Walter. *Gesammelte Schriften*. 8 Bde. Ed. Rolf Tiedemann and Hermann Schweppenhäuser. Contributing eds. Theodor W. Adorno and Gerschom Scholem. Frankfurt: Suhrkamp Verlag, 1972–1991.

———. *Illuminationen: Ausgewählte Schriften*. Compiled by Siegfried Umseld. Frankfurt: Suhrkamp Verlag, 1977.

———. *Illuminations*. Ed. Hannah Arendt. Trans. Harry Zohn. New York: Schocken Books, 1976 [1st ed. 1969].

———. *The Origin of German Tragic Drama*. Trans. John Osborne. London: NLB, 1977.

———. *Das Passagenwerk*. 2 Bde. Ed. Rolf Tiedemann. Frankfurt: Suhrkamp Verlag, 1983.

———. *Reflections: Essays, Aphorisms, Autobiographical Writings*. Ed. Peter Demetz. Trans. Edmund Jephcott. New York: Harcourt Brace Jovanovich, 1979.

———. *Selected Writings*. Vols. I–IV. Ed. Howard Eiland and Michael W. Jennings. Trans. Edmund Jephcott, et. al. Cambridge, Mass.: Harvard University Press (1996–2003).

———. *Ursprung des deutschen Trauerspiels*. Frankfurt: Suhrkamp Verlag, 1978 [1st ed. 1963].

Goethe, Johann Wolfgang von. *Gedenkausgabe*. 24 Bde. Ed. Ernst Beutler. Zürich: Artemis Verlag, 1950.

———. *Werke*. 14 Bde. Hamburg: Christian Wegner Verlag, 1955.

Hegel, G. W. F. *Theorie Werkausgabe*. 20 Bde. Ed. E. Moldenhauer and K. M. Michel. Frankfurt: Suhrkamp Verlag, 1977.

Heidegger, Martin. "Die Frage nach der Technik." In Heidegger, *Vorträge und Aufsätze*, pp. 5–36. Tübingen: Verlag Günther Neske Pfullingen, 1967 [1st ed. 1954].

———. *Identität und Differenz*. Dual-language edition. Trans. Joan Stambaugh. New York: Harper & Row, 1969.

———. *Platons Lehre von der Wahrheit: Mit einem Brief über den Humanismus.* Bern: Francke Verlag, 1947.

Hölderlin, Friedrich. *Sämtliche Werke: Grosse Stuttgarter Ausgabe.* Ed. Friedrich Beissner and Adolf Beck. Stuttgart: W. Kohlhammer Verlag, J. G. Cottasche Buchhandlung, 1943–1985.

Kant, Immanuel. *Kritik der praktischen Vernunft* (*KpV*). Bd. 6 in Kant, *Werkausgabe*, ed. Wilhelm Weischedel. Frankfurt: Suhrkamp Verlag, 1968.

———. *Kritik der reinen Vernunft* (*KrV*). Bde. 3–4 in Kant, *Werkausgabe*, ed. Wilhelm Weischedel. Frankfurt: Suhrkamp Verlag, 1968.

———. *Kritik der Urteilskraft* (*KU*). Bd. 10 in Kant, *Werkausgabe*, ed. Wilhelm Weischedel. Frankfurt: Suhrkamp Verlag, 1968.

———. *Werkausgabe.* 12 Bde. Ed. Wilhelm Weischedel. Frankfurt: Suhrkamp Verlag, 1968.

Lanzmann, Claude, dir. *Shoah.* Les Films Aleph, 1985.

Lessing, G. E. *Sämtliche Schriften.* 23 Bde. Ed. Karl Lachmann and Franz Muncker. Stuttgart: Göschen, 1886–1924.

Plato, *The Republic.* Vols. 5 and 6 of *Plato.* Dual-language edition. Cambridge, Mass.: Loeb Classical Library of Harvard University Press, 1982 [1st ed. 1930].

Proust, Marcel. *À la recherche du temps perdu.* 3 vols. Paris: Gallimard, 1954.

Rousseau, Jean-Jacques. *Discours sur l'origine et les fondements de l'inégalité parmi les hommes: Discours sur les sciences et les arts.* Paris: Flammarion, 1993.

———. *Du contrat social.* Paris: Garnier-Flammarion, 1966.

Saussure, Ferdinand de. *Cours de linguistique générale.* Paris: Payot, 1972.

Secondary Literature

Adler, Jeremy. *"Eine fast magische Anziehungskraft": Goethes Wahlverwandtschaften und die Chemie seiner Zeit.* München: C. H. Beck Verlag, 1987.

Adorno, T. W. "Zur Schlussszene des Faust." In *Goethe im XX. Jahrhundert: Spiegelungen und Deutungen*, ed. Hans Meyer, pp. 330–37. Hamburg: Christian Wegner Verlag, 1967.

Agamben, Giorgio. *Homo Sacer: Sovereign Power and Bare Life.* Trans. Daniel Heller-Roazen. Stanford, Calif.: Stanford University Press, 1998 [Einaudi, 1995].

———. *Remnants of Auschwitz: The Witness and the Archive.* Trans. Daniel Heller-Roazen (New York: Zone Books, 1999).

An, Jang-Hyok. *Goethes "Wahlverwandtschaften" und das Andere der Vernunft.* Würzburg: Königshausen & Neumann Verlag, 2004.

Aulhorn, Edith. "Der Aufbau von Goethes 'Wahlverwandtschaften.'" In *Goethes Roman "Die Wahlverwandtschaften,"* ed. Ewald Rösch, pp. 337–85. Darmstadt: Wissenschaftliche Buchhandlung, 1975 (orig. pub. 1918).

Barnes, H. G. "Bildhafte Darstellung in den 'Wahlverwandtschaften,'" *Deutsche Vierteljahrsschrift* 30 (1956): 41–70.

———. *Goethes Wahlverwandtschaften*. Oxford: Oxford University Press, 1967.

Barnouw, Jeffrey. "Faust and the Ethos of Technology." In *Interpreting Goethe's Faust Today*, ed. Jane K. Brown, et. al., pp. 29–42. New York: Camden House, 1994.

Berman, Marshall. *All That Is Solid Melts into Air: The Experience of Modernity*. New York: Penguin Books, 1988 [1st ed. Simon & Schuster, 1982].

Bersier, Gabrielle. *Goethes Rätselparodie der Romantik. Eine neue Leseart der "Wahlverwandtschaften."* Tübingen: Max Niemeyer Verlag, 1997.

Binswanger, Hans Christoph. *Geld und Magie: Deutung und Kritik der modernen Wirtschaft anhand von Goethes Faust*. Stuttgart: Edition Weitbrecht, 1985.

Blackhall, Eric. *Faust's Last Speech*. London: The University of London Institute of Germanic Studies, 1984.

Blessin, Stefan. *Erzählstruktur und Leserhandlung: Zur Theorie des literarischen Kommunikation am Beispiel von Goethes Wahlverwandtschaften*. Heidelberg: Carl Winter Universitätsverlag, 1974.

———. *Goethes Romane: Aufbruch in die Moderne*. Paderborn: Schöningh Verlag, 1996.

———. *Die Romane Goethes*. Königstein: Athenäum Verlag, 1979.

Böhme, Gernot. *Goethes Faust als philosophischer Text*. Baden-Baden: Die Graue Edition, 2005.

Böhme, Hartmut. "'Kein wahrer Prophet': Die Zeichen und das Nicht-Menschliche in Goethes Roman *Die Wahlverwandtschaften*." In *Goethes Die Wahlverwandtschaften*, ed. Gisela Greve, pp. 97–123. Tübingen: edition discord, 1999.

Bolz, Norbert W. "Ästhetisches Opfer. Die Formen der Wünsche in Goethes *Wahlverwandtschaften*." In *Goethes Wahlverwandtschaften: Kritische Modele und Diskursanalysen zum Mythos Literatur*, ed. Norbert W. Bolz, pp. 64–90. Hildesheim: Guttenberg Verlag, 1981.

Brandes, Peter. *Goethes Faust: Poetik der Gabe und Selbstreflexion der Dichtung*. München: Wilhelm Fink Verlag, 2003.

Brandstädter, Heike E. *Einfall der Bilder: Ottilie in den Wahlverwandtschaften*. Würzburg: Königshausen & Neumann Verlag, 2000.

Brandstetter, Gabrielle. "Gesten des Verfehlens. Epistolographische Aporien in Goethes *Wahlverwandtschaften*." In *Erzählen und Wissen: Paradigmen und Aporien ihrer Inszenierung in Goethes "Wahlverwandtschaften,"* ed. Gabrielle Brandstetter, pp. 41–62. Freiburg, i.Br.: Rombach Verlag, 2003.

Brodsky, Claudia. "Architectural History: Benjamin and Hölderlin." In "Benjamin Now: Critical Encounters with The Arcades Project," ed. Kevin

McLaughlin and Philip Rosen, special issue of *boundary 2*, vol. 30, no. 1 (Spring 2003): 143–68.

———. "Architecture and Architectonics: The 'Art of Reason' in Kant's *Critique.*" In *Canon*, vol. 3 of *The Princeton Journal: Thematic Studies in Architecture*, ed Taisto Mäkelä, pp. 103–17. New York: Princeton Architectural Press, 1988.

———. "The Coloring of Relations: *Die Wahlverwandtschaften* as *Farbenlehre.*" *MLN* Comparative Literature Issue 97 (1982): 1148–79.

———. "From the Pyramids to Romantic Poetry: Housing the Spirit in Hegel." In *Rereading Romanticism: Amsterdamer Beiträge zur neueren Germanistik*, ed. Martha B. Helfer, pp. 327–66. Amsterdam: Rodopi Verlag, 2000.

———. *The Imposition of Form: Studies in Narrative Representation and Knowledge.* Princeton: Princeton University Press, 1987.

———. "Remembering Swann: Memory and Representation in Proust," *MLN* Comparative Literature Issue 102 (1987): 1014–42.

Brodsky Lacour, Claudia. "Architecture in the Discourse of Modern Philosophy: Descartes to Nietzsche." In *Nietzsche and an "Architecture of Our Minds,"* ed. Irving Wohlfarth and Alexandre Kostka, pp. 19–34. Los Angeles: Getty Center, 1999.

———. "Narrate or Educate: *Le Père Goriot* and the Realist Bildungsroman." In *Approaches to Teaching Balzac's Old Goriot*, ed. Michal Ginsburg, pp. 32–44. New York: The Modern Language Association, 2000.

———. "The Temporality of Convention: Convention Theory and Romanticism." In *Rules and Conventions. Literature, Philosophy, Social Theory*, ed. Mette Hjort, pp. 274–93. Baltimore: The Johns Hopkins University Press, 1992.

Brosé, Claudia. "Park und Garten in Goethes *Wahlverwandtschaften*," in *Park und Garten im 18. Jahrhundert. Colloquium der Arbeitsstelle 18. Jahrhundert Gesamthochschule Wuppertal* (Heidelberg: Carl Winter Universitätsverlag, 1978), pp. 125–29.

Brown, Jane K. *Goethe's Faust: A German Tragedy.* Ithaca, N.Y.: Cornell University Press, 1986.

———. *The Persistence of Allegory.* Philadelphia: The University of Pennsylvania Press, 2007.

Brown, Jane K., Meredith Lee, and Thomas P. Saine, eds. *Interpreting Goethe's Faust Today.* New York: Camden House, 1983.

Buck-Morss, Susan. *The Dialectics of Seeing: Walter Benjamin and the Arcades Project*. Cambridge, Mass.: MIT Press, 1979.

Caygill, Howard. *Walter Benjamin: The Colour of Experience*. London: Routledge, 1998.

Comay, Rebecca. "Materialist Mutations of the *Bilderverbot*." In *Sites of Vision: The Discursive Construction of Sight in the History of Philosophy*, ed. David Michael Levin, pp. 337–78. Cambridge, Mass.: MIT Press, 1997.

Derrida, Jacques. *Moscou Aller-Retour*. Paris: Editions de l'Aube, 2005.

Dickson, Keith A. "Spatial Concentration and Themes in *Die Wahlverwandtschaften*." *Modern Language Studies* 1 (1965): 159–74.

Dworkin, Craig, *Reading the Illegible* (Evanston, Ill.: Northwestern University Press, 2003.

Elm, Theo. "'Wissen' und 'Verstehen' in Goethes *Wahlverwandtschaften*." In *Erzählen und Wissen: Paradigmen und Aporien ihrer Inszenierung in Goethes "Wahlverwandschaften,"* ed. Gabrielle Brandstetter, pp. 91–107. Freiburg, i.Br.: Rombach Verlag, 2003.

Faber, Richard. "Parkleben: Zur sozialen Idyllik Goethes." In *Goethes Wahlverwandtschaften: Kritische Modelle und Diskursanalysen zum Mythos Literatur*, ed. Norbert W. Bolz, pp. 91–168. Hildesheim: Gerstenberg Verlag, 1981.

Faets, Ann-Theres. *"Überall nur eine Natur"? Studien über Natur und Kunst in Goethes Wahlverwandtschafte*. Frankfurt: Peter Lang Verlag, 1993.

Fink, Gonthier-Louis. "Goethes 'Wahlverwandtschaften': Romanstruktur und Zeitstruktur." In *Goethes Roman "Die Wahlverwandtschaften,"* ed. Ewald Rösch, pp. 429–83. Darmstadt: Wissenschaftliche Buchhandlung, 1975 (orig. pub. 1971).

Flax, Neil M. "Goethe and Romanticism." In *Approaches to Teaching Goethe's Faust*, ed. Douglas McMillan, pp. 40–47. New York: The Modern Language Association, 1987.

François, Anne-Lise. *Open Secrets: The Literature of Uncounted Experience*. Stanford, Calif.: Stanford University Press, 2007.

Fries, Thomas. *Die Wirklichkeit der Literatur: Drei Versuche zur literarischen Sprachkritik*. Tübingen: Niemeyer Verlag, 1975.

Gearey, John. *Goethe's Other Faust: The Drama, Part Two*. Toronto: University of Toronto Press, 1992.

Gelley, Alexander. "Contexts of the Aesthetic in Walter Benjamin." *MLN* 114 (1999): 933–61.

Gould, Robert David. *Elective Affinities: An Investigation of the Influence of Goethe's Scientific Thinking on Die Wahlverwandtschaften*. Ph.D. Dissertation, Princeton University, 1970.

Hamm, Heinz. "Julirevolution, Saint-Simonismus und Goethes Abschliessende Arbeit am *Faust*." *Weimarer Beiträge* 28 (1982): 70–91.

Härtl, Heinz, ed. *Die Wahlverwandtschaften: Eine Dokumentation der Wirkung von Goethes Roman 1808–1832*. Berlin: Akademie-Verlag, 1983.

Heisenberg, Werner. "Die Goethesche und Newtonische Farbenlehre." In *Goethe im XX. Jahrhundert: Spiegelungen und Deutungen*, ed. Hans Meyer, pp. 418–32. Hamburg: Christian Wegner Verlag, 1967.

Heller, Erich. *Essays über Goethe*. Frankfurt: Insel Velag, 1970.

Hermann, Elisabeth. *Die Todesproblematik in Goethes Roman "Die Wahlverwandtschaften."* Berlin: Eric Schmidt Verlag, 1998.

Hielscher, Monika. *Natur und Freiheit in Goethes "Die Wahlverwandtschaften."* Frankfurt: Peter Lang Verlag, 1986.

Hölliger, Eva. "Das Motiv des Gartenraumes in Goethes Dichtung." *Deutsche Vierteljahrsschrift* 35 (1961): 185–215.

Hörisch, Jochen. "'Die Himmelfahrt der bösen Lust' in Goethes *Wahlverwandtschaften*: Versuch über Ottiliens Anorexie." In *Goethes Wahlverwandtschaften: Kritische Modelle und Diskursanalysen zum Mythos Literatur*, ed. Norbert W. Bolz, pp. 308–22. Hildesheim: Gerstenberg Verlag, 1981.

Horn, Eva, and Manfred Weinberg, eds. *Allegorie: Konfigurationen von Text, Bild und Lektüre*. Wiesbaden: Westdeutscher Verlag, 1998.

Kaiser, Gerhard. *Ist der Mensch zu Retten? Vision und Kritik der Moderne in Goethes "Faust."* Freiburg, i.Br.: Rombach Verlag, 1994.

Konrad, Susanne. *Goethes "Wahlverwandtschaften" und das Dilemma des Logozentrismus*. Heidelberg: Carl Winter Universitätsverlag, 1995.

LaCapra, Dominick. *History in Transit: Experience, Identity, Critical Theory*. Ithaca, N.Y.: Cornell University Press, 2004.

Lange, Victor. "*Faust: Der Tragödie zweiter Teil.*" In *Goethes Dramen: Neue Interpretationen*, ed. Walter Hinderer, pp. 281–312. Stuttgart: Reclaim, 1980.

Lockemann, Theodor. "Der Tod in Goethes 'Wahlverwandtschaften.'" In *Goethes Roman "Die Wahlverwandtschaften,"* ed. Ewald Rösch, pp. 161–74. Darmstadt: Wissenschaftliche Buchhandlung, 1975 [orig. pub. 1933].

Lukács, Georg. *Faust und Faustus*. Hamburg: Rowohlt Verlag, 1967.

Lützeler, Paul Michael and James E. McLeod, eds. *Goethes Erzählwerk: Interpretationen*. Stuttgart: Reclam, 1985.

Mehigan, Tim. "'From hence they resolve all Beings to Eyes': Zur Blickproblematik in Goethes *Wahlverwandtschaften*." In *Erzählen und Wissen: Paradigmen und Aporien ihrer Inszenierung in Goethes "Wahlverwandtschaften,"* ed. Gabrielle Brandstetter, pp. 169–85.

Mendelsohn, Daniel. *The Lost: A Search for Six of Six Million*. New York: HarperCollins, 2006.

Metscher, Thomas. "*Faust* und die Ökonomie: Ein literaturhistorischer Essay." In *Das Argument*, Sonderband 3 (1976): 28–155.

Mieszkowski, Jan. "Faust at War." Paper presented at the Annual Meeting of the American Society for Eighteenth-Century Studies, 2007 [forthcoming in *Germanic Review*].

Mieth, Günther. "Fausts letzter Monolog: Poetische Struktur einer geschichtlichen Vision." *Goethe Jahrbuch* 97 (1980): 90–102.

Mills, Catherine. "Playing with Law: Agamben and Derrida on Postjuridical Justice." In "The Agamben Effect," ed. Alison Ross, special issue, *Southern Atlantic Quarterly* vol. 107, no. 1 (Winter 2008): 15–36.

Muenzer, Clark. *Figures of Identity: German Novels of the Enigmatic Self.* University Park: Penn State University Press, 1984.

———. "Goethe's Gothic Classicism: Antecedents to the Architecture of History in *Faust II*, Act III." In *Interpreting Goethe's Faust Today*, ed. Jane K. Brown, et. al., pp. 187–206. New York: Camden House, 1994.

Murphy, Harriet. *The Rhetoric of the Spoken Word in Die Wahlverwandtschaften: Communication and Personality in the Novel.* Frankfurt: Peter Lang Verlag, 1990.

Nägele, Rainer. *Theater, Theory, Speculation: Walter Benjamin and the Scenes of Modernity.* Baltimore: The Johns Hopkins University Press, 1991.

Nemec, Frederich. *Die Ökonomie der Wahlverwandtschaften.* München: Wilhelm Fink Verlag, 1973.

Neubauer, John. "'Die Abstraktion, vor der wir uns fürchten.'" In *Versuch zu Goethe: Festschrift für Erich Heller*, ed. Volker Dürr and Géza von Molnár, pp. 305–20. Heidelberg: Lothar Stiehm Verlag, 1976.

Neumann, Gerhard. "Wunderliche Nachbarskinder: Zur Instanzierung von Wissen und Erzählung in Goethes *Wahlverwandtschaften*." In *Erzählen und Wissen: Paradigmen und Aporien ihrer Inszenierung in Goethes "Wahlverwandtschaften,"* ed. Gabriele Brandstetter, pp. 15–40. Freiburg, i.Br.: Rombach Verlag, 2003.

Niedermeier, Michael. *Das Ende der Idylle: Symbolik, Zeitbezug, "Gartenrevolution," in Goethes Roman "Die Wahlverwandtschaften."* Berlin: Peter Lang Verlag, 1992.

Noyes, John. "Die blinde Wahl: Symbol, Wahl, und Verwandtschaften in Goethes *Die Wahlverwandtschaften*," *Deutsche Vierteljahrschrift* 65 (1991): 132–51.

Öhlschläger, Claudia. "'Kunstgriffe' oder Poiesis der Mortifiation: Zur Aporie des 'erfüllten' Augenblicks in Goethes *Wahlverwandtschaften*." In *Erzählen und Wissen: Paradigmen und Aporien ihrer Inszenierung in Goethes "Wahlverwandtschaften,"* ed. Gabriele Brandstetter, pp. 187–204. Freiburg, i.Br.: Rombach Verlag, 2003.

Peucke, Brigitte. "The Material Image in Goethe's *Wahlverwandtschaften*." *The Germanic Review* 74.3 (1989): 195–213.

Radler, Rüdiger. *Goethes "Faust I" anders gesehen: Neue und visualisierte Interpretationen zu Grundfragen des Werkes.* Paderborn: Ferdinand Schöningh, 1995.

Reiss, Hans. *Goethe's Novels.* London: MacMillan, 1969.

Reusch, Judith. *Zeitstrukturen in Goethes "Wahlverwandtschaften."* Würzburg: Königshausen & Neumann, 2004.

Ricciardi, Alessia. *The Ends of Mourning: Psychoanalysis, Literature, Film*. Stanford, Calif.: Stanford University Press, 2003.

Riera, Gabriel. *Intrigues: From Being to the Other*. New York: Fordham University Press, 2006.

Ritzenhoff, Ursula, ed. *Erläuterungen und Dokumente: Johann Wolfgang Goethe. Die Wahlverwandtschaften*. Reclam, 2004 [2nd ed.].

Ryan, Judith. "View from the Summerhouse: Goethe's *Wahlverwandtschaften* and Its Literary Successors." In *Goethe's Narrative Fiction: The Irvine Goethe Symposium*, ed. Thomas Saine, pp. 145–60. Berlin: de Gruyter Verlag, 1983.

Scharf, Christian. *Goethes Ästhetik: Eine Genealogie der Schrift*. Stuttgart: J. B. Metzler Verlag, 1994.

Schell, Marc. "Money and the Mind: The Economics of Translation in *Faust*." In *MLN* German Issue 95 (1980): 516–62.

Schlaffer, Heinz. *Faust Zweiter Teil: Die Allegorie des 19. Jahrhunderts.* Stuttgart: J. B. Metzlersche Verlagsbuchhandlung, 1981.

Schlick, Werner. *Goethe's Die Wahlverwandtschaften: A Middle-Class Critique of Aesthetic Aristocratism.* Heidelberg: Carl Winter Universitätsverlag, 2000.

Schmitt, Carl. *Der Nomos der Erde im Völkerrecht des Jus Publicum Europaeum.* Berlin: Duncker & Humblot, 1997 [1st ed. 1950].

———. *Politische Theologie: Vier Kapitel zur Lehre von der Souveränität*. Berlin: Duncker & Humblot, 1954 [1st ed. 1922].

Schöne, Albrecht. *Fausts Himmelfahrt: Zur letzten Szene der Tragödie.* München: Carl-Friedrich von Siemens Stiftung, 1994.

Smith, Peter D. *Metaphor and Materiality: German Literature and the World-View of Science 1780–1955.* Oxford: Legenda, 2000.

Steer, A. G., Jr. *Goethe's Elective Affinities: The Robe of Nessus.* Heidelberg: Carl Winter Universitätsverlag, 1990.

Steinbiss, Jutta. *Der "freundliche Augenblick": Versuch über Goethes Wahlverwandtschaften*. Zürich: Artemis Verlag, 1983.

Steiner, Uwe. "Traurige Spiele—Spiel vor Traurigen: Zu Walter Benjamins Theorie des barocken Trauerspiels." In *Allegorie und Melancholie*, ed. Willem van Reijen, pp. 32–63. Frankfurt: Suhrkamp, 1992.

Steinhagen, Harald. "Zu Walter Benjamins Begriff der Allegorie." In *Formen und Funktionen der Allegorie. Symposion Wolfenbüttel 1978*, ed. Walter Haug, pp. 666–85. Stuttgart: J. B. Metzlersche Verlagsbuchhandlung, 1978.

Stöcklein, Paul. *Wege zum späten Goethe.* Hamburg: Marion von Schröder Verlag, 1949.

Suhrkamp, Peter. "Goethes 'Wahlverwandtschaften.'" In *Goethes Roman "Die Wahlverwandtschaften,"* ed. Ewald Rösch, pp. 192–214. Darmstadt: Wissenschaftliche Buchhandlung, 1975 (written 1944, orig. pub. 1951).

Sussman, Henry. *The Hegelian Aftermath.* Baltimore: The Johns Hopkins University Press, 1982.

Tantillo, Astrid Orle. *Goethe's Elective Affinities and the Critics.* New York: Camden House, 2001.

Thadden, Elisabeth von. *Erzählen als Naturverhältnis—Die Wahlverwandtschaften: Zum Problem der Darstellbarkeit von Natur und Gesellschaft seit Goethes Plan eines "Roman über das Weltall."* München: Wilhelm Fink Verlag, 1993.

Trunz, Erich, "Nachwort zu *Faust*." In Goethe, *Werke*. 14 Bde., III:463–96, Hamburg: Christian Wegner Verlag, 1955.

Twardella, Johannes. "Experimente im Triebhaus der Moderne: Versuch einer Kommunikationstheoretische Analyse von Goethes 'Wahlverwandtschaften.'" *Neophilologus* 83 (1999): 445–60.

Vaget, Hans Robert. "'Ein reicher Baron': Zum sozialgeschichtlichen Gehalt der *Wahlverwandtschaften*." In *Jahrbuch der deutschen Schillergesellschaft* 24 (1981): 123–61.

———. "Goethe's *Faust* Today: A "Post-Wall" Reading. In *Interpreting Goethe's Faust Today*, ed. Jane K. Brown, et. al., pp. 43–58. New York: Camden House, 1994.

Vazsonyi, Nicholas. *Lukács Reads Goethe: From Aestheticism to Stalinism.* Columbia, S.C.: Camden House, 1999.

Vogl, Joseph. "Nomos der Ökonomie: Steuerungen in Goethes *Wahlverwandtschaften*." "German Issue," *MLN* 114 (1999): 503–27.

Walzel, Oskar. "Goethes 'Wahlverwandtschaften' im Rahmen ihrer Zeit." In *Goethes Roman "Die Wahlverwandtschaften,"* ed. Ewald Rösch, pp. 34–63. Darmstadt: Wissenschaftliche Buchhandlung, 1975.

Weber, Samuel. "'The Principle of Representation': Carl Schmitt's *Roman Catholicism and Political Form*." In Weber, *Targets of Opportunity: On the Militarization of Thinking*, pp. 22–41. New York: Fordham University Press, 2005.

Wiethölter, Waltraud. "Von der Anstalt des Wissens und der Liebe zum eigenen Rock: Goethes *Wahlverwandtschaften*, enzyklopädistisch." In *Erzählen und Wissen: Paradigmen und Aporien ihrer Inszenierung in Goethes "Wahlverwandtschaften,"* ed. Gabriele Brandstetter, pp. 65–90. Freiburg, i. Br.: Rombach Verlag, 2003.

Winkelmann, John. *Goethe's Elective Affinities: An Interpretation.* New York: Peter Lang, 1987.

Wolff, Hans M. *Goethe in der Periode der Wahlverwandtschaften*. Berlin: A. Francke Verlag, 1952.

Zabka, Thomas. *Faust II: Das Klassische und das Romantische; Goethes Eingriff in die neueste Literatur.* Tübingen: Niemeyer Verlag, 1993.